Penguin Books
The Unprivileged

Jeremy Seabrook was born in Northampton in 1939.
He attended Northampton Grammar School, then
Gonville and Caïus College, Cambridge.
From 1962 to 1966 he taught at a secondary
modern school in Northampton, then at
Northampton Grammar School; and at this time he
was also a Workers' Educational Association lecturer.
Jeremy Seabrook went to the London School of
Economics in 1966, to study for his Diploma in
Social Administration. He was a social worker with
the Inner London Education Authority from 1967 to
1969 and is now a freelance writer. He researched a
film on children in the United Kingdom and Africa
for Kenneth Loach for a year – though the film failed
to get a showing. His play, *Life Price*, written with
Michael O'Neill, was put on at the Royal Court
Theatre early in 1969. He is the author of
City Close-Up (1971, also published in Penguins).

Jeremy Seabrook

The Unprivileged

A hundred years of family life
and tradition
in a working-class street

Penguin Books

Penguin Books Ltd, Harmondsworth,
Middlesex, England
Penguin Books Inc., 7110 Ambassador Road,
Baltimore, Maryland 21207, U.S.A.
Penguin Books Australia Ltd, Ringwood,
Victoria, Australia

First published by Longmans, Green 1967
Published in Penguin Books 1973

Made and printed in Great Britain by
Richard Clay (The Chaucer Press) Ltd,
Bungay, Suffolk
Set in Linotype Times

To My Mother

Contents

Foreword

For a long time my family passed on to each succeeding generation a knowledge of its history, its customs, ideas and values, and for as long as anyone can remember the transition from one generation to another had been accomplished without hiatus, as the received ideas were accepted and assimilated without question. But towards the middle of the twentieth century the process of transmission began to break down.

This book deals with the falling into obsolescence and decay of a way of life once believed by those who shared it to be the only admissible form that human life could take.

The material is drawn mainly from oral tradition, but I have supplemented it with my observations over a period of about twenty years. I cannot vouch for the accuracy of all the events, and do not accept responsibility for the judgements on past members of the family.

Some of the pieces have appeared in *New Society*, whose permission to republish I gratefully acknowledge.

J.S.

1. Oral Tradition: The Recital of Family History

In the year 1779 there was born in the parish of Long Buckby in Northamptonshire to the wife of a ploughman a male child. This child was never christened, to which omission some of the more superstitious of his descendants ascribe the awful happenings of his forty-ninth year, which is the earliest date still mentioned in the long oral tradition of our family. And if those events had been of a less shocking nature, it is likely that Joseph Timms would have been forgotten, as his parents were, and as indeed almost every other detail of his own life was. We know that he married a woman from Daventry, a Mary Muddiman. She bore him five children, the eldest of whom was called Ellen. This girl, who even now, a century and a half later, is still talked about only with shame and horror, bore him yet another child, likewise named Ellen, who has lain in Northampton Municipal Cemetery since 1913. In the isolated little red cottage on the thinly populated slopes around Long Buckby, denied the affection to which he considered himself entitled after his wife had finished childbearing, Joseph Timms seduced his eldest daughter, then a girl of nineteen.

When he could no longer bear the guilt and remorse, he drove out in a borrowed pony and trap to the highest hill in the county, where, following some secret expiatory ritual of his own, he ceremonially cut his own throat. After her husband's suicide, when the birth of his sixth and incestuous child could no longer be concealed, Mary rented a small sweet-shop in the main street of the little town, and lived a further twenty years to bring up Ellen and her daughter ostensibly as sisters, and distinguished by the names Nell (the elder) and Ellie (the younger). Nell spent not many more years in Long Buckby. At the annual fair she met a cattle-dealer called Lyman, who owned a large inn at Weston Favell, just outside Northampton, and who, on an acquaintance of two days, proposed marriage to her. She accepted, and immediately afterwards removed to Northampton. Although affronted by what she considered her daughter's desertion, Mary did not betray her. But she sighed and fretted in the little sweet-shop, and declared to her customers that God must have forgotten her, so long did He delay in calling her home.

Nell bore two children to Lyman, both of whom received a good education. The elder, who qualified as a medical practitioner, emigrated to New Zealand, where he is presumed to have died, for no more was heard of him after his departure. The younger, who was – and still is – known to the family simply as 'Son Lyman', died in Northampton asylum, and it is suggested by some of the older members of the family that he was put there out of the way by relatives who were anxious to possess themselves of his money. (He is said to have left more than thirty thousand pounds, inherited from his father, the cattle-dealer and hotel-keeper.)

As the years passed the family in Long Buckby dispersed, until at last Mary Timms died – called home during the parish aged persons' tea feast – and Nell requested of her husband that her younger sister Ellie be allowed to live with them, since with the removal from the sweet-shop she would be without a home. Old Lyman consented, and accordingly Ellie moved into the large stone house on the periphery of the town, to which he had elected to retire after concluding his business. For twenty years the secret of the relationship between the two women was guarded, and old Lyman suspected nothing. Only as she lay dying did his wife disclose the true nature of her relationship to the alleged sister. Before she died, she begged her husband to take care of Ellie, and, evidently rendered compliant by the prospect of imminent bereavement, this he promised to do. He altered his will, and left the money he had accumulated over the years to be divided evenly between his son and his wife's daughter, whom he had imagined to be his sister-in-law.

Family lore abounds in deathbed disclosures and posthumous revelations of secrets suppressed for years by wives in fear of violent and unpredictable reactions of husbands and fathers who allowed themselves all kinds of moral lapses, but who admitted of no such failings in their womenfolk. The women were obliged to keep silence, or they knew they might have found themselves turned out of the house, and they only unburdened themselves when death assured immunity from their husbands' anger.

Old Lyman survived his wife by only three years, and as soon as Son Lyman and Ellie had buried him, they moved into a small and squalid cottage close to the river, where they lived with a frugality unnecessary in view of the considerable amount of far more habitable property which they had jointly inherited. They are said to have lived on bloaters, and to have hidden a quantity of valuable spoons and plate under the floorboards of their tumbledown dwelling which was frequently flooded in winter, being at the bottom of the Nene valley. They were both graceless, austere and anchoretic, and the rare visits from kinsfolk were unwelcome and suspect. They knew that no one would venture through the long strip of clayey mud and rank grass that separated their dwelling place from the main road for the sake of any personal qualities they possessed. Dirt and silence were their only apparent characteristics, and they concluded, correctly, that anxiety about the ultimate devolution of their money must be the chief concern of their visitors.

To Joseph and Mary Timms were born four other children. The eldest lived next door to the sweet-shop, and all that is remembered of him is that his hair turned white overnight when his young wife died less than a year after their marriage. She died in childbed, and it is whispered that the child was not a child at all, but a creature with no eyes or nose, only a mouth that laughed and cried and clamoured for the breast during the few days of its life. Thomas Timms, my great-grandfather, was the nextborn of Joseph and Mary Timms. He made shoes on a bench in a small red-brick kitchen, and walked the eleven miles into Northampton twice a week to sell them and to collect more leather from the tanneries. He married a girl from

Buckby, called Mary Green, who is remembered as having
been a very pious and good-living woman, exceedingly fond of
the New Testament, but it is suggested that her piety was at
least in part an atonement for the one child she bore out of
wedlock, my grandmother. Mary Green always carried her
children with her on her right hip, with the result that by the
age of forty her hip-bone had become so displaced that she
limped, leaning heavily to the left as she walked. She outlived
her husband by more than thirty years. She went into mourning at the age of forty-six and never emerged from it. Mourning seemed to correspond to the sombre and desolate piety of
her disposition, and she entered weeds and crêpe as people
might enter a long-coveted haven or home. It was not that she
had been particularly devoted to her husband. Indeed, they are
said to have spent five years in almost complete silence after
some real or imagined infidelity of Thomas Timms with the
wenches as he sat on the long low bench in the sun outside
'The Wait for the Waggon' on his way to and from Northampton. He was idle and shiftless, and invented a sham blindness
as an excuse for neglecting his work, which his wife assured
him would 'find him out in the end', the pretence of such an
affliction being the surest way of bringing it upon himself.

The next child is remembered only for having lived to be
ninety-seven, his longevity having produced nothing more remarkable than itself. And even if it had, it would almost certainly have been overshadowed by the wicked life of his sister,
Hannah, the youngest child of Joseph and Mary Timms whose
name is recorded. Of course no enormity committed by the
offspring of such a man should surprise anyone. Most of his
descendants are in agreement about this. A kind of fatalistic
what-can-you-expect colours their attitude, although it must be
pointed out that they are less indulgent about the misdemean-
ours of their contemporaries, less inclined to account for them
by the sins of the fathers. They show almost total unanimity in
their demand for increased severity to combat present-day immorality or crime.

The greatest of Hannah Timms's crimes was to introduce
herself one Christmas as a temporary servant into the house-

hold of a 'Vicar's daughter' in the eighteen-fifties, in search of a refuge in which to give birth to and afterwards destroy an unwanted child. Responsibility for her pregnancy was lodged vaguely but firmly with 'the gipsies', as though they had, in their plurality, conspired to besmirch the honour and dignity of the family. (The gipsies were a constant scapegoat, and although the family always claimed to be imbued with an awareness of its lowly station in life, it was not so lowly that it was unable to derive a great deal of pleasure from the contemplation of those it imagined to be more lowly still, whether gipsies, criminals or foreigners.) In early January after Hannah Timms's crime, some labourers, who had been engaged to empty the privy, found the body of a male infant clumsily inhumed in the night-soil. A servant recalled that he had seen Hannah Timms a few days earlier in the wash-house, where she had appeared to be in the act of incinerating a bloodstained cloth. She did not deny that the child was hers, but she asserted that it had been stillborn. This was confirmed by the surgeon who had examined the body, and she was sentenced to six months' imprisonment for concealing the birth of a child. Her employer apostrophized the court in a most dramatic manner upon the pitfalls which beset anyone in those days contemplating the engagement of domestics without proper references, even for the briefest periods of celebration of holy festivals. It was less the illegitimate child which affronted her kinsfolk than the disrespect showed by implicating her parish priest in her crimes, and for this reason her reputation for depravity almost eclipsed that of her father.

The name of the youngest child of Joseph and Mary Timms is not remembered. What is remembered, and with much bitterness and resentment, is the fact that they had a daughter who married a man called Hawes; that Mrs Hawes in turn had a daughter who married an Arnold, a boot and shoe manufacturer. That, however, is not the cause of the bitterness. This is traceable to a dispute over the will of Son Lyman, under which a considerable sum would have been due to my grandmother Ellen (as well as a large house in what passed for the town's most select thoroughfare) if her brother Gus had not pointed out that since she had been born out of wedlock (notwithstanding the fact that her parents subsequently did marry, and that Mary Green became very fond of the New Testament in later life), she could not claim to be the nearest relative of the defunct Son Lyman. The family was nonplussed by this piece of treachery, and the money devolved upon Mrs Hawes, for reasons that were not explained to anybody's satisfaction. The loss of their anticipated fortune was accepted as being part of the necessary order of things, possibly because of the superior social standing of Mrs Hawes, against which they felt themselves too insignificant or too ill-informed to make any stand. The bitterness was aggravated by an offer made by one of the executors of the will to my grandmother of an advance of £1,000 upon the sum due to her. She had refused, protesting that she had lived for so long without two half-pennies to rub together that she might just as well wait until the whole sum became available. When she learned that the money was finally lost she comforted herself by saying that she had never believed in the legacy anyway, and that those born to be poor would always stay poor. Earlier Ellen had been urged to have the rich though unbalanced Son Lyman removed from the asylum by a far-sighted relative, who claimed to have foreseen her brother's treachery (the family produced many of these visionaries, whose horror at disasters of all kinds was considerably attenuated by the vindication of their prophecies which had always fallen on deaf ears), but since she was at the time living in a two-bedroomed house with nine children, she declared she wouldn't have known what to do with him. The lack of space was so acute that when one of her children died in infancy it had to be shut away in a drawer until the day of the funeral.

Thus family lore was coloured by resentment at what might have been, and shame at what most dramatically and irremediably had been. Children learned to assimilate this resentment at a very early age. The Sunday afternoon walks were turned irresistibly in the direction of the dingy villa that had been snatched from the family by Gus's malice. So great was the sense of grievance that, even when I was a child, long after the house had passed out of the hands of the usurpers, I felt a pang of hatred for the unknown occupants behind the heavy brocade curtains every time I passed by. I still considered their ownership provisional and reversible, and I still hoped that their trickery might one day be revealed and the house restored to the sad old woman with her astrakhan hat and elastic-sided black boots. But although the children were exposed to and encouraged to share the family's indignation, they were carefully screened from the family's shame. Indeed, so complete was the silence of all parents on sexual matters that, if it had not been for the inventiveness of children, no generation would ever have survived to produce another. Parents never believed in the sexuality of their children, and the onset of puberty or menstruation often seemed to shock parents as much as their sons and daughters.

To Thomas and Mary Timms were born six children: Ellen (my grandmother), Frank, Gus, Mary Ann, Fred, Ted and Laura. Each of these went into service as soon as they were of an age to leave home. At ten, Ellen was sent to her first 'place', in Eaton Square. Many years later she explained the apparently brutal removal of a girl so young from her family by the fact that it was not the custom for children to serve in houses locally, because it was felt that gossip carried back into the servants' families and streets might destroy the aura of mystery essential to the maintenance of prestige and social position. She was treated kindly in London, and was so small and frail a creature that her employer is said to have taken pity on her and to have re-united her with her family, although it must be pointed out that this did not happen until more than two years after her original departure. Her greatest sufferings were at the hands of the upper servants who mocked her gauche provincial accent and manners, and who sent her out one day to buy 'a silver new-nothing to hang on Mistress's arm'. She returned home and went to work in the lunatic asylum in Northampton. She had two vivid memories of this period: one was of sitting apart from the doctors and nurses, eating bread and dripping while they ate bacon and sausages, and the other of the groups of sightseers, who, on certain days and for a

penny, could clatter at will round the rusty iron balcony that
bordered a central hall in which the lunatics exercised themselves, or sat or screamed or defecated. Ellen had undergone a
brief and intermittent schooling in Long Buckby, where she
had once been given the salutary exercise of writing a hundred
times, 'I cannot see God, but God can see me.'

It was not suggested by anyone that any of the children of
Thomas and Mary Timms should do anything but serve, and
they of course submitted to the bending of their various personalities into this single direction without question or protest.
Indeed, to many of them their service was a source of pride. In
later life Mary Ann dwelt with great tenderness upon the rig-
ours of her first place. 'Ah, we was real servants in them days,
up at five in the mornin', cartin' buckets full o' coal up five
flights o' stairs. There was nothin' soft about us.' Many of
them merged their own insignificant lives with those of the
exalted beings they were called upon to serve. They had so
profound a sense of inadequacy and unworthiness that they
often identified themselves completely with their employers.
They would have thought it presumptuous to form independent opinions, even if they had had access to any information
beyond that which their masters saw fit to pass on to them.
Occasionally they absorbed a few resounding sentences and
maxims from those they served, which they would deliver
ponderously before their cowed relatives, believing them to be
sophisticated and trenchant comments on society, but which in
their plain discourse were exotic and out of place, like a sudden orchid blossoming in a municipal flowerbed. One of Ellen's
brothers was constantly saying 'Irreligion stalks the land', a
conclusion which he could not possibly have reached by himself, and which he uttered with a confidence borrowed from his
betters. Whenever he repeated it, which was frequently, it was
always greeted by a chorus of scandalized and deferential tut-
tutting.

The self-effacement which characterized them has to some
degree affected nearly all of their descendants. The feeling of
abasement, which they were taught was the virtue of humility,
has left a legacy of social unease, and a complete inability to

deal with those of a different social background. The precise modulations of a schoolteacher's voice, the self-assured inflexions of a doctor or minister can still send the hand fluttering nervously to the stray lock of hair, and cause the colour to rise in old men, as they detect, even in the kindest words, traces of the voice born to be obeyed. Even when they had moved into the town and worked in the boot factories many of them displayed an archaic exaggerated respect for their employers, and they would sometimes prowl round the factory, spying out shirkers or apprentice-boys wasting time and urging them indignantly to 'get their hands out of the boss's pocket'.

Ellen's oldest brother, Frank, is remembered as having served with the Elwes family, who finally dismissed him for drunkenness. Of his days in service he retained, even in the cramped house in Scarletwell Street, Northampton, a predilection for polished silver and the whitest of napery, and he is reported to have laid the scrubbed deal table as for a banquet at every meal, even when – as was frequently the case – there was nothing to eat. He suffered all his life from asthma, and he put an end to it by throwing himself under a train at the age of sixty. His daughter Alice, whose reputed ill-health showed no sign of improvement in all the eighty-seven years of her life, was a creaking gate, whose most cherished possession was a medical book full of grey speckled photographs of women with Eton crops and cancer, and his younger child, Bill, is famous for having gone out one afternoon to post a letter, and never having been heard of again.

Fred, the next child of Thomas and Mary Timms, had eight children: Tom, George, Alfred, Annie, Ada, Lou, Nell, Emily. This is said to be the most unfortunate family in the whole elaborate memory-system of our kin. As soon as war was declared in 1914 all three sons enlisted together, vehement and febrile in their hatred of the enemy. Their mother never saw them again. She learnt of their deaths with composure and resignation, claiming that she had known on the first day, when she had seen the long lines of men in civilian clothes and bowler hats marching to the railway station, that they had gone for good. Although they did not believe her, nobody said

so, allowing her the meagre consolation of faith in her own
powers of prophecy and foreknowledge. Within six months
nothing remained of them but the patriotic songs and poems
meticulously copied into their sentimental sisters' albums:

> I'll go one, said Belgium,
> I'll go two, said France,
> I'll go three, said the Japanese,
> I think I stand a chance.
> I'll go four, said Germany,
> And wipe you off the map.
> Then up rose old John Bull and said,
> Well dammit, I'll go nap.

> Be a soldier, be a man, be a hero, I know you can
> And remember, boys, when you're marching to war,
> It's a grand old country that you're fighting for.
> When you're facing shot and shell,
> To your birthright lads be true,
> And do as your father did before you,
> In the days of Waterloo.

Alf's wife died in childbirth, Ada was consumptive and Lou's
two husbands were both killed in the war, which proved to
some of the superstitious members of the family that it wasn't
meant to have more than one husband, although this scarcely
accounted for the premature death of the first, permissible,
one.

Ted was my grandmother's youngest brother. He is described
by those who remember him as a thin pathetic man, who for
many years sold muffins in the streets of Kettering from a
wicker-basket covered with a cloth. He was ineffectual and
improvident, and died in the workhouse, to the shame of all
his relatives, who, immediately after this embarrassing event,
broke into abuse and imprecation against each other, less from
a genuine concern about the unhappy end of Ted, than from a
fear that other people might judge adversely this failure to
carry out their duty to a kinsman. His wife used to go 'ash-
boxing', an unworthy and discreditable occupation, to which
few members of the family ever descended even in the hardest

times, and which involved foraging for food and firewood in
the dustbins outside the big houses. She always wore a greasy
black coat, and she walked with such a stoop that it brushed
the ground before her as she went. She pushed an old pram,
which she used as a support for her frail and unsteady legs
rather than as a receptacle for her spoliation of the dustbins of
the rich. Ted had two daughters. Gertie, the elder, died of
tuberculosis at the age of twenty-three, while Edie 'married
well', and consequently passed out of her relatives' range of
vision.

Laura, youngest of the children of Thomas Timms, was also
the luckiest, as was often the case with the lastborn. She became a schoolteacher at the instigation of the family with
whom she served. When she joined them at the age of twelve
they were impressed by her intelligence and resourcefulness,
and they paid for her education. She taught at first in Long
Buckby, and later in Leicester, where she met Will Moss, likewise a schoolteacher, whom she married. She, living at the
great distance of thirty miles, acquired the reputation of being
a rich relation, and it is true that she may have owned a sooty
red-brick villa, with stained glass in the front door and a bell
that you pulled like a lavatory chain, on the outskirts of
Leicester, but she was later found to be 'in the moneylenders'
hands', for most of the family a more opprobrious fate than
any sexual crime.

About 1880 Ellen, my grandmother – named in defiance of
the misery it had brought her aunt – had the misfortune to
marry against the advice of every right-thinking member of the
family, who 'would rather have seen her in her grave than wed
to Edwin Youl'. He was what they euphemistically termed 'a
wrong 'un'. And once that has been said there is little more to
add. He drank, he was dishonest and generous, brutal and attractive. Stories of his cruelty still abound. They remember how
he would come home from the pub and drag his wife on to a
pile of sacks in the corner of the room after he had driven out
all the children except Billy, who 'hadn't got all his buttons'
and was therefore allowed to witness everything that happened, he being considered unlikely to understand its signifi-

cance. Soon she would be in the family way again, unless she 'got rid of it', a mysterious and crude operation, to which she had frequent recourse, and in which it was later disclosed a knitting needle and 'the carbolic' played a significant part. She was afraid of her husband, and this had to be carried out in the greatest secrecy, although it is unlikely that he did not know of her actions. He simply insisted upon being shielded from all evidence of them. On the picture-rail he kept a thin brass stair-rod, and this was used for ceremonial beatings of the children, and sometimes of his wife, although with her he generally contented himself with the back of an open hand. One night he came home from the pub with a woman, and roused the children from their sleep to ask them what they thought of their new mother. Ellen dressed them hurriedly and took them out of the house, and they spent the whole night on one of the ornamental green-painted iron benches in the park.

Like most of the men of his generation Edwin Youl was taciturn and uncommunicative. A few ritual phrases constituted the only oral contact between him and his wife, and he displayed a complete indifference to the children, except when he felt called upon to punish them for some misdemeanour or other. On these occasions, as well as the stair-rod, he had a wide range of blood-curdling threats, which he was fortunately never known to carry out, but which he uttered in language of primitive brutality and crudity. 'I'll cut your bloody heart out of you.' 'I'll cut you bit from bit.' The cruelty of all our menfolk was felt to be of great disciplinary value in the formation of their children, a view with which many of the children in later life concurred, as they dwelt with rueful affection upon the chastening corrective battery of straps, rods and canes, which they confidently claimed had taught them right from wrong.

Edwin Youl was a skilled clicker, but he worked only sporadically, and parted very grudgingly with every penny he gave his wife. A large part of her life was taken up with contriving meals and clothing with inadequate money. She would cite examples of her inventiveness and resourcefulness with great pride and triumph, as though she were talking of some enemy she had outwitted, as indeed in a sense she had, for privation and poverty were for her a necessary part of existence itself. In 1895, at the time of the lockout in the boot and shoe industry, her husband had given her no money for six weeks. She took her eldest child, Lill, into the fields, and showed her where to find a kind of edible snail she knew. They collected half a pail full of these and took them home for the family's consumption. They had to be soaked first in salt water for twenty-four hours to remove the slime and grit, and then they were boiled. Nobody seemed to find this dish in any way exceptionable. Sometimes, however, even her ingenuity failed her, and she used to tell how she would put the children to bed at three o'clock in the afternoon, and pull some sacking over the window to simulate night, so that the children should sleep and not feel hunger. Her life was peopled with bailiffs and creditors and rent-men and women from the various 'strap-shops' she used (which had to become increasingly distant from her home, as the knowledge of her inability to pay became more widespread). She displayed great skill in evading or thwarting them, hiding in cellars or cupboards (although Lill answered the door one day and ingenuously informed a creditor that her mother had unaccountably locked herself in the cellar), and once she even persuaded her next-door neighbour to swear to a creditor that she had been taken to the madhouse the day before.

She was completely without bitterness, possibly because she had no social awareness at all. She accepted such discrepancies as she observed between the lives of rich and poor as the most natural thing in the world. Sometimes she would recite this rhyme to her children, but not with any intention of inspiring them with radical or revolutionary ideas:

> Dimes and dollars, dollars and dimes,
> To be poor is the worst of crimes.
> You can be rogue or knave or fool,
> But don't be poor, it's against the rule.

She submitted to poverty in the same way that she submitted to her husband's bullying and cruelty. She did not in fact distinguish between the two. They were both manifestations of some incomprehensible and impenetrable force which moulded and shaped her life, and in which any personal intervention would have been unthinkable.

Edwin Youl's 'conversion' came late in life. All his children had grown up in fear and disliking of him, distrusting the exaggerated bouts of beery tenderness that alternated with his cruelty, and learning from a very early age that there was no reciprocation in their relationship with him, the same action being likely to provoke an indulgent boozy grin one day and a beating with a stair-rod the next. The conversion didn't exactly happen overnight, but between the ages of fifty and sixty he became transformed with a Scrooge-like thoroughness. The vindictiveness and surliness disappeared, and his grandchildren benefited from the affection and tenderness which he had withheld from his own offspring. The latter were always very sceptical about his change of personality, but there was no doubt that it was genuine. They felt inclined to ascribe it to belated religious scruples or the onset of senility. Ellen was convinced that the Good Lord had made him mend his ways, but since she had been brought up on tracts and tales about drunkards and outcasts and strays and fallen women who had all renounced their evil ways from one verse to the next, she saw nothing implausible in her husband's transformation, although occasionally she would look at him apprehensively, as though his unwonted mansuetude were perhaps merely another refinement of his cruelty, and his real personality were about to declare itself at any moment with renewed vehemence and intensity.

All Ellen's children began work in a boot factory. Just as her generation had gone unquestioningly into service in the eighteen-sixties and eighteen-seventies, so at the end of the century all automatically gravitated towards the factories. First came Lill, who began at the age of eleven, and who married Alec Warren, a farmworker from Naseby. The second child was Joe, who began work at the age of twelve, and became a console operator. He was bitter and intolerant, one of the rare politically conscious members of the family. The war, where he lost an arm and a leg, he often declared to have been the happiest time of his existence. He had a passionate and undifferentiated hatred for everything foreign, and he talked with great disgust of the Jerries, the Froggies, the Ities, the Chinks and the Japs. He remembered the Chinks particularly from the war. They used to go round with a little bowl tied to their waist, and they used to drink from it, eat out of it and then shit in it, which fact he would flourish as conclusive proof of their sub-human nature. His hatred extended to the Catholics, the Jews, the pansies, and especially, in the last years of his life, the blacks. He refused to go out, protesting that as soon as he stepped outside the front door he no longer knew whether he was in Northampton or Zululand. Earlier he had been accustomed to sing at Christmas gatherings, in his rare moods of expansiveness and geniality, a song he had been taught at Sunday School:

> Over the sea there are little brown children,
> Fathers and mothers and babies dear.
> No one has told them about the Lord Jesus,
> No one has told them that He is near.

But with the first appearance of immigrants in the town this affecting hymn vanished abruptly from his repertoire. As a corollary of his xenophobia, he had a mystical and extremely sentimental idea of England. He was full of hortatory rhymes:

> Whatever you are – be that;
> Whatever you do – be true;
> Straightforwardly act – in fact
> Be nobody else but you.
> Your character true unfurl,
> And when it is ripe
> You'll then be a type
> Of a Capital British Girl.

The limbs he had left at Passchendaele he had relinquished as a kind of pledge of the value of his beliefs, and as he grew older he grew more deeply entrenched in the extravagant patriotism that had seized him in 1914. He became a grotesque anachronism, and died in the conviction that Hitler had failed only because this country had ignored the divine mission to which it had been called, and had refused to throw in its lot with its own flesh and blood. After the First War he married Elizabeth Jones, daughter of a boot and shoe operative. He was, however, an inveterate womaniser, and it was for many years a family joke that the loss of his limbs had not in any way diminished his sexual capacity. It was not regarded as a joke by his wife, and she finally took her own life by gas. She became for a time quite celebrated for having been one of the first people in the town to do away with herself in that particular way, and her funeral cortège was swelled by a number of curious people, who found the novelty of the cause of her death an irresistible reason for attending her burial.

My grandparents' third child was Maud. She developed an early sense of the inadequacy of her social background and its values. As a girl she once saw 'King Teddy' – as she still affectionately calls him – on an official visit to Northampton racecourse; she was so close to him that 'she could have touched him', and this fleeting proximity to so great a personage seemed to enhance permanently her own social status. She came under no influences different from those to which her sisters were exposed. She knew nobody from any other milieu. And yet she learned to be ashamed of the house next to the rag-and-bone shop, and her mother's constant battle against the fleas and cockroaches and flies and bugs that held the house in perpetual siege. She made a long detour to reach her school, so that no one should see her emerge from the back streets. She acquired a neutral accent that made even her most matter-of-fact observations sound like carefully rehearsed recitations. For the rest of her family the rag-and-bone shop, the pawned clothes, the violence and the bread and lard were the most natural things in the world, and the only contrasting ideal they knew was not a social one, consisting as it did of shining mansions and bridal feasts and streets of jasper and garments of white. But Maud had somehow acquired *social* knowledge, like a precocious and more shocking puberty. Later she was able to cultivate her inclinations towards gentility and 'refinement', which showed themselves in chintzy interiors and brass ornaments and biscuit tins covered with pictures of royal residences and doorbells that played the opening bars of 'Santa Lucia', and an intimate knowledge of the vicissitudes of all the great English ducal houses in the last hundred years. It may have been a surfeit of stories in childhood about wistful orphans in charity institutions who turned out to be heiresses to titles and fortunes, cheated of their birthright by malevolent kinsfolk, but it is far more likely that the ideas she professed sprang from her own temperament and personality. Maud had always been by nature reserved, gentle and pacific, and it was natural that life in the streets, which was none of these things, should drive her to find its antithesis. Of course she was accused of snobbery and standoffishness. In the family's words, 'She thought the sun shone out of her arse.' The notion that what are popularly termed 'bourgeois' and 'proletarian' characteristics are purely a product of social conditioning may be false. It may be that they correspond instead to a fundamental cleavage in human personality, and it only happens that a majority of one or the other finds itself in one particular group.

The fourth child, Laura, having ceased formal education at twelve, started work in an outdoor closing establishment, and she married Bill Cansdale, a sole-sorter in the rough-stuff room of a large boot factory. By the time Ethel, the fifth child, was due to start work, an Act of Parliament had deferred the age of this significant step in their lives to thirteen. She worked in a closing room, and married Arthur Megeary, a painter and decorator, who had been called in to give the dingy house in Green Street its first coat of paint in living memory. They removed to Olney in North Buckinghamshire early in the 1920s, when Arthur could no longer find work in the town.

Ellen's next child was Billy, who died in infancy, and was therefore not claimed by the factories. A good deal of mystery surrounds his birth and death. It is said that he was 'big-headed', but all her life his mother passionately denied that he was in any way abnormal. Sometimes she suggested obliquely that 'the strength wasn't given him', or that 'he was too good for this world', but even if the boy had been obviously defective in any way – like Mrs Turland's Dottie, whose head was so heavy that she was unable to hold it erect and had to let it droop forward with its mass of wild yellow hair on to her thin chest like a great overblown flower – Ellen would have refused to acknowledge any flaw in a creature to which she had given birth. It was not that she could have been oblivious of his weakness; it was simply that it had to be concealed from outsiders. When Billy was about four his sister was dressing him one day. So that she could reach him more easily she set him down in the hearth, and did not realize that he was sitting on some live cinders that had fallen through the bars of the high grate. Although he was naked, he did not cry out, and a large patch of flesh was seared before his sister noticed that anything was wrong. Some time later she was heard telling this story to a neighbour's child, commenting that Billy wasn't clever enough to know that he was being hurt by the live coals. As a result she received a rare beating from her mother. It was possible to acknowledge such things within the family group, but to mention them outside was unthinkable. Parents and children frequently disliked each other, and their relationships were often sour and joyless, but in public their notions of 'motherhood' or 'parental affection' made them proclaim the perfection and excellence of their kin to all-comers. Within the privacy of the family children never ceased to be reproved for their ingratitude, husbands were constantly taxed with selfishness, but as soon as a stranger appeared they were transformed into beings of flawless and unimpeachable virtue. Ellen was frequently heard to affirm that Billy was 'the best thing that ever happened to her', although in reality she had little patience with his slow-wittedness and his inability to learn.

Ellen's seventh child was Harry. He began as a sole-cutter at the age of thirteen, but later became a tanner. He never married, in spite of a courtship that lasted ten years. Of them it was said that 'One was frit, the other daren't.' He lived at home until his mother died. At the age of eighty-seven Ellen was knocking down plums with a line-prop from the tree which had stood in the back garden ever since anyone could remember. She fell down and broke her thigh, and spent thirteen weeks in hospital before succumbing to pneumonia.

The womenfolk had always danced a most slavish attendance upon their men. In the house the men did nothing. They were not expected to carry the coal or to chop sticks or to carry the dustbin through the house to be placed on the pavement for collection. The preparation of a cup of cold strong tea on rare Sunday mornings marked the extreme limit of Edwin Youl's tenderness towards his wife, and even this simple chore involved the use of every piece of crockery in the house and put him in a bad humour for the rest of the day. When Edwin came home from work his chair had to be vacated immediately. He would throw down his kit-bag and coat on the floor for her to pick up, and without a word he would sit down and lift each boot in turn for her to undo the laces and pull them off, resting his foot as he did so on the darned and faded pinafore that she always wore in the house. His meal had to be set before him at the precise moment when he was ready for it, and as this would vary from day to day it was something she had to be able to anticipate intuitively. If it failed to appear at the right moment he would say, 'Where's me bloody tea, woman?' and that would be the sole extent of his conversation until he had eaten, which he did noisily and voraciously, liberally splashing with gravy the newspaper that had been placed beneath his plate to keep the table clean. As he ate, she would keep up a monologue about the day's happenings, to which he paid no attention at all, and when he had finished he would retire behind a racing paper until he fell asleep or until it was time for him to go out. When he died, the attention which he had received all his life devolved upon the only male then living at home.

The men were always treated with the greatest deference, less from a genuine respect than from a fear of their arbitrary and capricious changes of mood and sudden outbursts of violence. Edwin Youl frequently hit his wife, generally with the back of an open hand, and she always pretended to be hurt more badly than she was. Otherwise, she confessed, he might have killed her. Once, when I was very young and my brother and I had been left at the house, Ellen and her husband had a violent quarrel. He struck her, and she fell across the floor. He tried to revive her, but she would not open her eyes. We were in the garden, and, attracted by his cries – he was shouting in an attempt to resuscitate her – we ran to the window. (He had locked the door.) We stood staring at the pantomime of his efforts to bring her back to life, and the growing panic of his gestures and demeanour. Once she had let things go so far she could not allow herself too abrupt a revival for fear of provoking his anger yet further. If she recovered now there would be no limit to his violence. She had to wait until his panic gave way to terror at the damage he had inflicted. At length he became lachrymose and remorseful. He raised her up gently on to the leather sofa, and he even addressed her by her Christian name – a very rare thing for either of them. Under normal circumstances they called each other 'man' and 'woman' in the vocative case, and reserved the use of first names for times when they wanted to show tenderness or affection, which occurred only during serious illnesses or when they became afraid of losing each other. Habit had bound them together. It was not that they complemented each other, or that the relationship enriched or fulfilled either of them. Their lives would undoubtedly have been better apart. But Ellen's suffering and the insults which she had received at the hands of 'that man' had become so much part of her that without them she would have been at a loss to furnish her existence. Even if he had not stolen her rent money from under the clock to buy beer, if he had not pawned the coat that one of her sisters had passed on to her, if she had had a sober and industrious husband, she would still have found, in the perfection from which she felt herself excluded, some cause for complaint and regret.

Two years after Harry, Win was born. Until now all the children had been christened, but by this time birth had become so frequent an event in the family, and Ellen was so exhausted, that she no longer bothered. Registration of births was deferred to the latest moment – so late in fact that dates had to be falsified to avoid a contravention of the law, and nine-month-old infants had to be passed off as newly born. For many of them the celebration of a birthday is an arbitrary event, a day chosen somewhere near the actual anniversary, but seldom accurate, a kind of official birthday – like royalty. They were nearly all given monosyllabic names, plain and unpretentious (unlike the following generation, who tended to bear the names of heroes and heroines of films which their mothers had enjoyed during pregnancy). They were always addressed with the prefatory 'our', our Win, our Dick, our Lill, possibly to distinguish them from anybody else's Lill, Dick or Win, for so numerous were the families and so few the names considered suitable that nearly everybody had a Lill, Dick and Win, and without the possessive adjective all kinds of confusion and misunderstanding might have arisen. Win began work at thirteen. She later married a man called Edward Robinson, who operated a press in the rough-stuff department of the same factory.

Dick followed Win, and he was said to be 'delicate'. For this reason he was accorded the privilege of trundling a Co-op delivery cart for twelve months, the idea being that this period in the fresh air would set him up for life. Whether his brief spell exposed to the weather helped to make possible the subsequent thirty-five years which he spent in a shoe-factory cannot, of course, be known. He had the reputation of being a deep thinker, a very doubtful compliment in our family, who believed that it led to morbidness and melancholia, and who generally inclined to the view that social and political questions were not worth bothering about, since 'Everything will still be the same in a hundred years' time.' It was felt that it was all very well knowing what had happened a thousand years ago, but when this excluded any knowledge of the scandalous remarks that Mrs Perkins had made yesterday about Mrs Watt's Teresa, then it was taking things a bit too far. Dick was a reserved and gentle man, earnest and anxious as he haunted reading-rooms and public libraries ('always non-fiction' whispered the family to each other in awe, as though this were proof of unparalleled erudition) in search of the education that had been denied him. He assimilated a vast but fragmented and unrelated collection of knowledge, and he remained bewildered that his sense of inferiority in the presence of educated or cultivated people did not diminish at all. The few members of the family who gave serious consideration to politics or to abstract ideas were always suspect. Their wives, exasperated by or jealous of their socialism or trade union activities, would complain that it gave them the creeps, and quite often they took vengeance upon their menfolk by proclaiming allegiance to the Conservative cause. Their vote was as likely to be a product of marital discord as of deep conviction.

Ellen's tenth child was Emily. She began work knot-tying in 1912 in a factory that was obligingly burnt to the ground during her second week there. She married Frank West, who contracted tuberculosis in the Royal Navy, and she nursed him until his death in 1949.

May was Ellen's eleventh child in fourteen years. She bore children as a tree bears fruit, passively, effortlessly. Once a woman arrived at her door and claimed to be carrying in her belly a child of Edwin Youl's. Ellen smiled at her and said, 'You're lucky, I've carried ten.' May was one of the most intelligent members of the family. At the age of thirteen she passed an examination which in principle entitled her to be transferred to the High School for Girls. On the day of her triumph she ran home from school and burst into the house, crying, 'Mam, Mam, I'm going to the High.' Her mother looked at her and said, 'Are you, me duck?', and May knew at once from the expression in her voice that such a thing was out of the question. And the next day Ellen took her by the hand and led her down to the factory, where a job was found for her at her sister's side, tying the same knots. Both girls encountered a good deal of cruelty in the factories. May started work the week before the August Bank Holiday. In the room where she worked shoes were piled in pairs up to the ceiling. She was told that she would have to match them all with laces before she would be allowed to go on holiday, and she was found by the cleaners after everybody else had gone home, crying over an endless tangle of shoelaces on the finishing-room floor.

The youngest child, Gladys, left school at fourteen, but began work in the office of a boot-factory, favoured by the fact that many of the family were self-supporting by this time, and that she was not therefore obliged to accept the first job that presented itself. Although the youngest of the family, she was at the same time its most representative member, having been her mother's favourite (in spite of Ellen's boast that she 'never made fish o' one and fowl o' the other'), and therefore more inclined to accept the ideas and outlook of an earlier generation. She was in a sense archaic, the final repository of a great body of family lore and tradition, as well as of many country customs and superstitions already falling into desuetude, but still preserved by her because they emanated from her mother. Well into the nineteen-sixties every summer she would spend months preserving fruits and pickling vegetables and making jam and wines, because this had been done by all female members of the family for as long as anyone could remember. The fact that the corner shop was now stacked from floor to ceiling with those very things she was preserving did not suppress in her the same urgency that earlier generations had experienced when they saw the trees heavy with ripe fruit and the sun declining earlier each day in the afternoon sky. She would have felt herself to be idle and wasteful if she had allowed the abundance of plums and apples on the market stalls and the elderberries and blackberries in the hedgerows to disappear without capturing at least some of them in her innumerable preserving jars, which she did with the delight and tenderness of a child who consigns a rare and precious butterfly to a matchbox.

The upbringing of the children was accomplished with only sporadic parental intervention. They descended like gods in a classical tragedy only for events of a fairly momentous nature – to mete out punishments or pieces of advice rendered portentous and oracular by mysterious references to their 'experience'. This experience, which they invoked to interpret or explain away any event that occurred, stood them in the stead of actual knowledge. It meant that they had known want, witnessed death and seen a certain amount of human suffering. But all this penetrated their consciousness and then simply lay there, heavy and unproductive as a stone. They imagined that

experience itself, independently of its significance, qualified
them to pass judgement on anything under the sun.

Ellen's youngest daughter was so deeply imbued with the
idea of family loyalty and continuity that she knew the whole
of the family's story word for word, as though its perpetuation
in every detail had been formally entrusted to her. In a sense it
had. As the oldest member of one generation passed on her
knowledge to the youngest of the next, it became more than a
mere recital of the accumulated pride and shame. There was
something else – perhaps an unformulated hope that the secret
knowledge running through the years like a great underground
river might one day reach the surface, somehow vindicating
the family's hidden unknown existence to those who governed,
led and taught them, and who knew nothing of their alien
values. Once the Town Missionary visited a member of the
family who was close to death. In his record of the visit to the
dilapidated house in Bath Street he wrote: 'This man has been
afflicted a long time, and a few months ago had his arm ampu-
tated at the Infirmary. The disease appears still in his body and
he seems to suffer much pain. I have had some reason to hope
that a favourable change of mind has taken place. I spoke to
him of the probability of his soon being called away, and the
opportunity given him by a lingering disease of making his
peace with God.' They did not derive their real beliefs and
ideas from people for whom they represented nothing more
than service or labour, abstractions, but fell back instead upon
a very ancient peasant tradition, of which echoes are still
heard today.

2. Ideas

Birth, marriage and death were always treated with the greatest ceremony. Stories of deaths which occurred only two or three generations ago tell of fires being extinguished and mirrors turned against the wall and all perishable foods thrown away (although it generally was ensured that all such foods were transferred to the house next door when death became imminent, where it was considered to be in less danger of contamination by the passing of a human soul). There was once a fierce quarrel over a deathbed, where the patient's death-rattle was prolonged to such an extent that one of the watchers at the bedside suggested that it might be the tightly shuttered windows which prevented her from dying properly. She was clearly struggling for release, and if the window were opened she would die without difficulty. The sister retorted that since it was mid-January nothing would be more certain than death for all of them if they exposed themselves to the blizzard. The window was opened and closed several times before the patient died. One of the two women was able to ascribe the death to the beneficent action she had performed in facilitating the soul's departure, while the other declared it to be nothing more mysterious than pneumonia.

Human life was so important that the whole natural world was subservient to it, and betrayed constant portents and warnings and clues about the future for anyone who knew how to interpret them. It was remembered that blossom had appeared on the plum tree in the autumn of the year before my grandmother died, a sure sign of approaching death. For them nature had a profound meaning for human life, not, as for the Romantic poets, in the imagined harmony between its moods and their own, but in the innumerable omens and indications to be found there foreshadowing the future. It was possible to anticipate a death, to predict the course of a marriage or the progress of a newly born child from conditions prevailing in the natural world at the time of an illness, a wedding or a birth. The world had for them a wholeness and coherence which it has since lost. It was not Arcadian or sentimental. The real fear in which their superstitions held them – and at least fifty common phenomena were considered certain fore-runners of death – was a grim and joyless feature of their lives. But everything had meaning. The flight of a bird, the flowering of the trees, the colour of the moon represented something more than mere scenery to be stared at uncomprehendingly for its picturesqueness through a car window on Sunday after-noons. There was a profound connection, not always pleasant or beneficent, between human life and the most insignificant wild flower or the smallest insect. Corn-poppies induced sleep and blindness, drooping blossoms introduced into the house presaged death. I remember as a child my mother's sudden, bewildering anger one day when I picked up some trampled daffodils abandoned on the muddy cobbles from a market flower-stall. 'Pick up a flower, pick up sickness,' and she thrust them vigorously from me into the gutter. My grandmother, seeing a solitary crow perched on the clothes-line, would prophesy a death before the week was out. And since she al-ways turned immediately to the deaths columns in the local paper every evening, she rarely had much difficulty in estab-lishing a link between some omen and the death of someone she knew.

Even the fire burning in the grate – ancient elemental source of so many superstitions – was frequently consulted as an in-fallible means of divination. If the fire burned at the first match your love was said to be burning brightly or your sweetheart smiling. If the fire burned itself out at the centre, leaving a hollow surrounded by half-consumed coals or wood, this meant certain death to someone in the household. The old women who no longer moved from the fireside restlessly fin-gered the poker, ready to destroy unfavourable omens in the hearth. As the cinders fell through the horizontal bars into the fire-basket, they were closely examined: if they were short and square they represented cradles, or births; if elongated they stood for coffins. Sparks flying up the chimney were souls going to heaven; sparks flying out into the room showed that someone was 'having his spite out on you'. When a shred of soot-covered plaster fluttered in the draught at the back of the fireplace a stranger would soon arrive at the house, and when the flame burned blue frosty weather could be expected. These were not simply quaint or curious superstitions, deferred to absent-mindedly, out of habit, in the way that some people touch wood or throw salt over their shoulder: these were of crucial significance in their whole view of the world. Almost every manifestation of nature presaged or symbolized something else. And because those who believed in them believed with such conviction they were a great source of strength. They united the family in an unshakeable faith far more effectively than formal religion. In later generations, as the universal superstitions became weakened and finally suppressed, private and incommunicable neuroses burgeoned in their stead. Their irrational beliefs were like a hereditary poison, which, if it no longer manifests itself in blains and pustules on the surface of the skin, none the less continues its toxic effects insidiously and invisibly. Previously there had been no one like Aunt D., who was persecuted by everyone in the street, spied on as she ate, watched as she sat on the lav, whose house was entered at night by people intent upon rearranging her furniture and playing her piano. Cousin G., with her imaginary pregnancies and empty tumescent belly, became a figure of fun to all those who could not understand the nature of her suffering, and who, when they were not making mock-solicitous inquiries about her condition, were telling her to pull herself together or to snap out of it.

Ellen Youl, like everyone else of her generation, knew that the moon shining on the face of a sleeping child was likely to cause madness. When her children had warts, they could be charmed away by being rubbed with some meat that afterwards had to be buried. As the meat rotted in the earth, so the warts would disappear. (Although if she had been as poor as she was reputed to be, some of her descendants uncharitably suggested, she ought to have found a better use for any spare pieces of meat with a dozen children to rear.)

A bird tapping at the window, a picture falling from its hook for no obvious reason, a dog howling on its chain throughout a long summer afternoon, a bat at dusk thudding against a dusty window-pane, all these things warned of approaching death. Meat handled by a menstruous woman would go bad. During the last war the family was scandalized by the fact that my mother looked after a butcher's shop unaided by any male, and for this reason custom diminished appreciably. For many years no member of the family would go to the Co-op because of 'all them gals handlin' the meat when they're like that. . . .' If you ate from a plate resting upon another you were drowning a sailor at sea, and if the wind changed while you were pulling faces you would be left with the disfiguring rictus for life. There was a vast and complicated network of relationships between apparently unconnected events and phenomena: if a farmer burned holly his cows would go dry, if you deliberately killed a spider you would never 'live and thrive'. Sheet lightning ripened the corn, cow-dung used as a poultice cured boils and abscesses, a potato under the mattress was proof against rheumatism, and such beliefs were the last vestiges of a way of life in complete harmony with natural surroundings.

There remained many pagan superstitions, sometimes absorbed or sanctioned by Christian custom, submerged fragments of a faith that remained hidden but not ousted for many years after its apparent supersession by more rational ideas, and upon which they could still draw at times of great stress or suffering, combating with a kind of pagan mysticism all they did not understand. A cousin called May died in infancy. The mother bestowed the same name upon her next-born, a defiant and ill-advised thing to do, for everybody knew that the dead May would call her namesake away. And it was true that the second May was a weak and sickly child. Her constant pining and fretting were attributed to the baleful influence of her dead sister who, it was felt, wanted a companion. It was considered a wonder that she lived, although as soon as twelve months had passed the mother claimed that she was beyond the reach of her dead sister's malevolence. It was strange that a child, upon whom, for as long as she lived, every attention and care had been bestowed, became a force of evil, something to be feared and appeased, when she died. Their notion of what happened after death often showed a complete disregard for the teachings of the religion to which they sometimes claimed to defer, as in this instance, where even the name of a dead child could destroy a living one. When death occurred they would enact the prescribed rituals, and accord the necessary ceremony to the burial of their dead, but this did not always involve their basic beliefs, which often went deeper. When a cousin was killed in a motor-cycle accident a few years ago, his mother went into a shop after the funeral and bought him a new leather coat. It was felt that she had been unhinged by grief, but she herself knew what she was doing, and felt obscurely that he might have need of it.

They had always been preoccupied with death. The old aunts still sit in the churchyard the whole summer long, reading the epitaphs and watching the flowers fade on newly risen mounds and wondering who's going to be next. They all claimed to believe in God, and the nearest they ever came to metaphysical doubt occurred when a particularly young or vigorous member of the family died. Then they would gather at the funeral and say elliptically, 'It makes you wonder...', and although they never finished the sentence, everybody understood what was meant. A boy of nine died of tetanus, having cut his hand on a rusty nail, and they expressed sad reproachful doubts about God's goodness, although this did not stop the insertion of 'God whispered Michael and called him home' in the local newspaper. In the family there was a cousin who had devoted fifteen years of her adult life to an ailing mother. At length the mother died, and Vera, who was then thirty-three, met a man whom she later married. But the intercourse started up a dormant cancer of the ovaries, and within nine months of marriage she was dead. This time-sequence seemed to them of a hideously cruel and ironic significance. Not only had she effaced herself all her life and submerged all her own personal existence in the service of her mother, she had 'kept herself pure', saved herself, and in the time it takes for a human child to develop, this monstrous thing grew inside her body and killed her. They gathered at her funeral, bitter and silent and puzzled. 'She hadn't had her life', 'She was no age at all'. Helplessly they assailed the incomprehensibility of life, but they still left the door open after the departure of the funeral procession, so that the spirit should be able to take its leave without difficulty of the place where it had dwelt.

Beside their professed belief in God there existed in many of them an equally profound faith in 'the spirits' – and these were something quite separate from the malign powers of dead children. Often they would visit a Spiritualist Temple or a Demonstration of Clairvoyance, clutching a wedding-ring or watch belonging to the deceased, in the belief that this would facilitate communication. They were always disappointed, feeling themselves constantly on the brink of contact with their dead, but this feeling may have been due to the peculiar intensity in the transmission of family traditions, which created an illusion of proximity to long-past generations. Ellen's daughter May had the reputation of being a particularly forceful personality, and she made a solemn promise to come back from the dead if it were at all possible. When she died her sisters agreed that if she couldn't find a way back nobody ever would, and accordingly, half-doubting yet apprehensive, they attended a number of spiritualist meetings, carrying a brooch and a locket belonging to the dead woman in their handbags. They were disappointed, but at the same time secretly relieved when contact failed to be made. They admitted afterwards that if their assignation with their dead sister had been achieved, they would have been at a loss for something to say, and they talked of it as of some embarrassing social encounter, triumphantly though narrowly avoided, as though death had somehow enhanced their sister's social standing. Exasperated wives frequently threatened their husbands that they would return to haunt them after having been driven to an early grave, and the idea was quite widespread that your defunct kinsfolk were watching over you on high, guiding, approving or censuring your conduct, although there is little evidence of their tutelary interest having decisively influenced the course of anyone's life.

None of them ever doubted life after death. This was not really surprising. The consumptive young wives, the sons who didn't come back from the war, the children who died of a mysterious and unspecified 'fever', would have made nonsense of their lives if they had not believed that death represented a continuation of the many truncated and incomplete relationships of their earthly existence. Preoccupation with contriving meals, keeping a job, obtaining credit, precluded the luxury of deep and rewarding relationships, and the family was full of people who reproached themselves half a lifetime for not having appreciated a mother or sister while she lived. There had been no time. And the image they had of life after death was a direct and idealized extension of their daily life. Paradise meant the possibility of developing relationships left unconsummated, and sometimes even barely begun, in spite of forty years of married life or three decades spent in the parents' home. They were so convinced of the purely physical extension of their life that they would sometimes speculate upon where everybody went. 'Well, I wonder where they put you all?', 'they' possibly becoming confused in their mind with the hosts of employers, administrators of the poor-law, workhouse officials who had figured so largely in this life. It was going to be a kind of evacuation, and to a real place in a precise geographical location, perhaps even with tickets of identity tied to the wrists, like the holidays of slum children to converted country houses, an outing to the mansions of the blest, which were Victorian Gothic in style, and not very different from the great houses of boot manufacturers in the town's most superior streets. There was to be a physical reunion with their loved ones, which may have been an agreeable prospect for a family as large as ours, but which could have afforded little pleasure to those who were alone. If any thought was given to such people, it was assumed that they would probably band together like people who don't know each other

at a party. They even had fairly precise ideas as to their style
of dress:

> Around the throne of God a band
> Of glorious angels ever stand
> Bright things they see, sweet harps they hold
> And on their heads are crowns of gold.

The degree of blessedness to be enjoyed in the next world was
felt to be in direct proportion to the amount of suffering endured in this one. This conviction was disturbed only by occasional anxiety as to how they would actually spend their time
when they reached it, unrelieved blessedness evidently not
being considered a sufficient pursuit in itself with no variety or
distraction. 'What are we going to do all the while?' they
would ask, as they projected into eternity memories of prolonged wet Bank Holiday weekends, the tedium of nothing to
do, the impatience for work to begin again.

Hell had only a shadowy and peripheral existence in their
universe, and to it they consigned only a handful of people,
those who were deemed to be of monumental and unrepentant
evil – Hitler or Crippen, or men who 'interfered' with children.
They certainly did not think of anyone they knew or had ever
known personally as worthy inhabitants of hell. It may be that
actual contact with other human beings, and the admittedly
elementary insight into their motives and behaviour which
such contact afforded them, blurred somewhat the inflexible
standards of right and wrong by which they claimed to regu-
late all their judgements. Of course every member of the family – even those who in life had been qualified as 'wrong 'uns' –
was dispatched unhesitatingly to heaven. As relatives died,
children were urged to append an ever amplified codicil to
their prayers, invoking God's blessing on Grandma, Auntie
Maud or Uncle Joe 'in heaven', which phrase they stressed
meaningfully, as though in exhortation to whoever might be
listening to rectify any omissions or errors that had occurred.
It was widely believed that those who died became all-pervad-
ing celestial spectators of human life, from whom there could

be no secrets. In this way grandmothers, who had been harmless in life with their nodding heads and the whiskers on their chin and their sweet deaf uncomprehending smiles, were transformed into a kind of ubiquitous ghostly policeman, whose help was unceasingly summoned by weak or indolent parents in the control of their children.

Resignation characterized their attitude towards life, and they were only sustained by an incontestable belief in some fundamental though unrevealed cosmic justice. 'It was sent.' And they believed that the life of each individual is made up of an equal amount of hardship, joy, suffering, pleasure. The ostensible disparity between the lives of people merely indicated the submerged nature of those equalizing factors they knew to exist. Justice will always be established sooner or later, wrong always atoned for, good inevitably rewarded. ' 'Tain't long,' Ellen would say, folding her hands confidently over her darned pinafore, ' 'tain't gunner be long 'fore I see all them as 'ave shit on me an' rubbed it in punished for their wickedness.' She was convinced that she would be a triumphant witness of the downfall of the woman who had persecuted her from the strap-shop, the pawnbroker who had taken advantage of her poverty and despair. Many of them believed that justice was not confined to heaven, but would also invariably be established on earth, and when confronted by evidence to the contrary – as when children died, or cheats, in defiance of their constantly recurring dictum, manifestly did prosper – they did not allow their beliefs to be undermined. They may have voiced an occasional and hesitant doubt, but they preferred in the long run the comfort of unshakeable convictions to frequent disturbing reassessments of their position, and all doubts became in retrospect merely symptoms of weakness. 'It'll find you out in the end' was their cry. If you told a lie your tongue would drop out, if you took something that did not belong to you, your fingers would stick to it, and although such ideas are perpetuated today only in the lore of children—as in the threat to the unmoved child who says 'I don't care' that Don't Care was hanged, or the threat that if you masturbate your hair will drop out and you will go mad, or the idea that if you throw bread on the fire you are feeding the devil – only a few generations ago these beliefs prevailed in every age group.

The conviction that every human being knew joy and sorrow in equal measure often enabled them to derive some comfort from the misfortunes of the rich: they would stand all day waiting for the funeral cortège of local gentry or factory owners so that they could make sententious remarks about equality, as though the fact of the mortality of the rich somehow attenuated their own poverty and privation.

Their idea of justice was as cruel and inflexible as the laws which at one assize alone in Northampton less than a century and a half ago could sentence twenty-eight men and women to death. Still strong is the belief that natural calamities – earthquakes, storms, floods – are a direct consequence of human wrongdoing. At the time of the Skopje earthquake in 1963 the family's country-dwellers were unanimous in their declaration that 'it must be caused by some folks' wickedness somewhere'. It had to be accounted for. With those who still work on the land an inclement season calls forth the same strictures on increasing crime and lawlessness. Human transgression is likely to be visited with punishment in unpredictable and apparently unconnected ways. Sexual crime may blight the crops or result in the death of an innocent child. The phenomenon of the adulteress abandoning her lover as soon as her child begins to show symptoms of serious illness was familiar to the family. They are not easily brought from this conception of justice. The crops do fail, and children do die. The belief in causal links between seemingly unrelated phenomena could not be discarded without destroying the completeness and coherence of their world. When they are confronted with inexplicable death or suffering they will search anxiously for some event within their own immediate experience to account for it, and in their need they will sometimes ascribe it to things in no way commensurate with the degree of suffering involved: a farm or street accident may come to be blamed upon insistent demands for higher pay in industry. It is another act of hubris, another example of people getting too big for their boots, and consequently responsible for all kinds of unhappiness and misery.

Recently an old kinsman, whose allotment had been ravaged by a neighbour's dog, said that he had prayed and prayed that the neighbour should be punished for his carelessness. 'And he was. You know that big wind we had a couple o' weeks back? It was sent. It blew his garden shed down.' For them human justice should be a clear and unaltered reflection of what they believe to be 'natural justice'. Death is the only answer to murder. Violence must be met with even greater violence. Those guilty of sexual crimes should be castrated. At family gatherings they will advocate punishments and reprisals of medieval savagery, public whippings, stringing them up, birching them and rubbing salt in the wounds. At such times their talk is full of Old Testament echoes, and their vocabulary assumes an exotic Biblical colouring, with words like 'sin', 'shame', 'sorrow' freely used – words which have long disappeared from their everyday conversation. Whenever any member of the family is found to have committed any crime or misdemeanour they become still more stricken and portentous, and it is surprising that the high incidence of shotgun weddings and extra-marital pregnancies never resulted in any diminution of the righteous horror and incredulity with which they were greeted. And yet, in spite of an ostentatious display of moral outrage at such things, in practice they showed a surprising ability to accommodate a wide range of deviation from their proclaimed and allegedly inflexible standards. It is astonishing how soon the presence of an illegitimate child or the lapses of a womanising husband came to be accepted without comment. As generation followed generation their concessions to received moral values became more and more perfunctory – an obligatory piece of ritual, a superstition. They dutifully mounted a display of shock and disapproval at a daughter's pregnancy, but adherence to their frequently affirmed principles was confined to a few months' querulousness and abuse, and then it was forgotten. The business of preparing for the child, arranging a marriage for the girl – 'getting her to church before she fell to pieces' – caused the principles to fall into abeyance. They became an irrelevancy, like unrepealed though obsolete laws, which nobody has the courage to abrogate officially for fear of appearing to connive at poaching the king's deer or withholding an annual silver groat from the poor of the parish. None of the family would have liked anyone to think that they were without clearly defined notions of what was 'proper' or 'right'; it was simply that in reality these had very little bearing upon their conduct, and personal exigencies, individual relationships were seldom inhibited by deference to 'accepted' moral standards if they happened to depart from them.

Nothing interposed itself between the family and the transmission of its beliefs and superstitions from generation to generation. Children were impregnated with them from an early age, and the process of transference was osmotic. The fears and taboos penetrated everything, and the young assimilated them by a kind of contagion. There was nothing calculated in the perpetuation of ideas. It was simply taken for granted that they would be conveyed, intact, like an heirloom or treasure. I remember how the obscure disquiet of my mother and grandmother at any death-omen communicated itself to me in their troubled expression or restless anxiety. I could not believe that their dark unease could be without cause, and I came to be filled with the same foreboding. It was a far more efficient and enduring process than any formal indoctrination. The first time I left home for a fairly long period I turned back for something I had forgotten, not knowing that having once left the confines of the home, to return is a sure indication of disaster. The family was convinced that I would never come back alive, and they broke into angry imprecation against my thoughtless infraction of this taboo for anything so trivial as a pair of forgotten sunglasses. Their distress and concern affected me to such an extent that I almost abandoned my journey – which at one level was certainly the purpose of their nevertheless genuine fear: no one was ever encouraged to leave the family group, for however brief a period, and expose himself to alien ideas. This explains some of our prejudice against those who sought to educate us, and it was not, as our near-sighted and petulant teachers often claimed, a perverse and wilful refusal of their wisdom. We had been taught to resist everything, even when it was something as indisputable as noun clauses or the sum of the square on the hypotenuse.

It was only a hundred and fifty years ago that the last known attempt was made in Northamptonshire to ascertain the guilt or innocence of a woman suspected of witchcraft by throwing her into the river, and of course with us, too, such deeply rooted beliefs could not be cast off with indifference. My great-aunt had a daughter who was simple-minded. She would sit on the doorstep sadly watching the clumsy, elephantine girl, and swear that she had been 'overlooked' when she had been with child. Nothing would convince her that the girl's affliction was not the direct result of a neighbour's malevolence. When pressed to reveal the identity of the malefactor she would close her lips tightly and shake her head and say it would be more than her life was worth. One or two older members of the family still assert that they are able to work harm against those they dislike simply by the power of their will. 'Anybody as has crossed me,' Aunt Poll used to say solemnly, 'I'm only gotter wish sommat on 'em, and sooner or later, you can believe it or believe it not, but sommat 'll 'appen to 'em.' Sometimes she even claimed to be afraid of her own power, and whenever misfortune befell anyone she knew, she would remember some occasion on which she had had cause to wish them ill. Momentary impatience with a child crying in the street late one night led to its contracting a fatal disease. Aghast at what she had done, she tried to make amends by showing herself full of solicitude and kindness for the bereaved mother. She surprised and embarrassed the afflicted woman by presenting her with an elaborate expensive wreath. The surprise and embarrassment were intensified by the fact that Poll was renowned for her meanness and since she had scarcely ever spoken to the family in question apart from some trifling complaint, her gift was even more unaccountable.

One kinswoman who had a child with a club-foot believed

that she was being punished for something she had done wrong. She could not imagine what her crime or sin had been, but this did not diminish her sense of guilt. Of course when children misbehaved or were ungrateful it was a frequent histrionic gesture for their mothers to call them a punishment or 'their cross', but in this case there is no doubt that her bewilderment was real. And as a result she expended upon her son an overwhelming expiatory affection, which made him even more dependent upon her than he might otherwise have been, and when she died he survived her by less than a year. Similarly, when Ellen's husband ill-treated her – when he struck her or failed to come home at night – she would ask what she had done to deserve a man like that. Everything that happened to them had to be understood in terms of reward or punishment, and it sometimes seemed that the crippled child or Edwin Youl had no more human reality than their afflictive or compensatory rôle in the lives of those around them. Edwin Youl had been sent for no other reason than to try her. With such a view it is not surprising that she never made any effort to understand him. His alcoholism was only considered in so far as it related to her own life. Its destructive and corrosive tyranny over her husband did not concern her, and her repeated magnanimous pardons were intended only to contrast her own virtue with his wanton depravity. The possibility that she and her husband had simply chanced to meet and had made an unsuccessful marriage would have been quite unacceptable. Nothing was gratuitous. Nothing came to disturb the order and meaning of her life, even if violence had to be done to reality before it conformed to that preconcerted order and meaning.

Although they were all convinced that they had been 'put there' for a purpose (a purpose which they never ventured to define and which it often wasn't 'given to us' to understand in our ignorance), their lives were in fact so uncertain and insecure in every way that many of them sought refuge in the spurious reassurances of fortune-tellers and the stars. Nearly all of their superstitions connected with the natural world were warnings of imminent death, sickness or loss, and they sometimes needed to be comforted by the belief that legacies and dark strangers and rich relatives were not crowded out of their future by the suffering and hardship which they all anticipated, and which, they affirmed grimly in a rare and sombre concession to anything resembling a sense of humour, it didn't need a fortune-teller or a soothsayer to foretell. As late as the eighteen-eighties an aunt was fined for telling fortunes for money to gullible young girls who used to throng into her tiny back kitchen. Everybody agreed that she had been unfairly dealt with. After all she had only told them what they wanted to hear – an occupation which has since that time become a major industry. She had two outlandish characteristics which set her apart from the rest of the family. She took snuff and had been a dresser at the Palace of Varieties, where she acquired an outrageously tolerant and permissive 'it-takes-all-sorts' attitude towards life, which enabled her to joke about adultery or prostitution at a time when these were proscribed topics in the family, or only mentioned amid an elaborate pantomime of horror, mouthed silently across the parlour over the bowed heads of children. It was sometimes suggested that her liberal views stemmed from some irregularity in her own make-up, for she was referred to as a 'man-kind sort o' woman', a term used to denote a virago, and Edwin Youl only spoke of her as 'that bloody ole horse-godmother'. Whenever she dwelt upon the beauty or charm of any of the stars she had met, the conversation was always abruptly deflected into other directions, particularly if any children happened to be within earshot.

Tom N., a distant cousin, claims that his deliverance from harm in the Great War was entirely due to the stars. 'We'd be all camping out in a tent, eighteen of us. I'd say to 'em, "Come on, boys, over this side. Don't sleep over there." And they'd all move over to one side o' the tent, and sure enough a shell'd come in the night and go clean through it.' He is full of premonitions. 'There was this lad, Second War I'm talking about now, flying in the R A F. Me and mother met him on leave. He was with his girl. He said that night he was due to go over Germany. I said, "Give 'em one for me while you're at it." The minute we left him, we hadn't gone two yards and I felt this pain right across my forehead. I said, "Mother, that boy won't come back." She said, "Why don't you go an' tell him?" I didn't know whether to or not. He was killed that night. I could have been killed a dozen times myself. They used to laugh at me. One night we were in a hut, bitter cold night, I wouldn't go in. They all laughed. I had a cold night, but I was the only one as lived to see the next day. They was laughin' the other side their face then. The hut was shelled in the night. All dead.'

He is not at all disturbed by the knowledge so mysteriously vouchsafed him about the future. None of the family's prophets or diviners ever was, and it used to surprise me that their lives were outwardly no different from anyone else's. They did not use their knowledge to advance themselves materially, and they were nearly all poor, resentful and querulous about not being heeded. The truth was that Tom had a sombre and pessimistic turn of mind, and his premonitions of disaster were so frequent that he could scarcely have failed to be right at least sometimes. He foresaw the death or downfall of everybody he knew at least once a day, and in view of this it is surprising that his reputation for accurate predictions should have come to be so respected.

In the formation of their ideas and opinions and beliefs they were subjected to so many haphazard and contradictory influences that their outlook was often inconsistent, compounded as it frequently was, of shreds of superstition, half-understood aspects of Christianity, fragments of ancient ritual and custom. For them the notion of 'freedom' had very little meaning. They were as they were by accident, adventitiously, passively. If they had embraced their idea of the world as a conscious act of choice, fully understanding at the same time all those things they were rejecting, then they could perhaps be said to have done so freely. But in fact the alternatives were never placed before them. They yielded to circumstances as the conifers on Cley Hill yielded to the prevailing wind and leaned towards the east. They contracted their social values like an infection from those around them. They were in thrall to their past, and they continued to enact the rituals and traditions of a way of

living defunct and without meaning. Just as they had preserved in their speech words and idioms of Anglo-Saxon origin
which had been lost to the standard tongue, so they had retained in their lives customs and habits of thought that had
become congealed and ossified until no one any longer knew
their original significance. For instance, at a funeral it was
always imperative to leave the front door ajar so that the spirit
of the dead person would be able to leave the house at its
leisure – it was somehow felt that the spirit might choose to
linger on the premises in order to view the body it had inhabited, and, being distracted like a careless butterfly by something of interest in the house, might fail to notice the departure of the funeral party and become inadvertently locked
in. (As though this conventional means of egress were the only
one a spirit could devise, and it never seems to have occurred
to anyone that it might be able to seep through semi-porous
brick or fly up the chimney if necessary.) When the custom of
keeping the body in the house between the point of death and
the time of the funeral was discontinued, the practice of leaving the door open remained, and even the theft of thirty shil-
lings from a vase on the mantelpiece during the inhumation of
a great-aunt did nothing to weaken the ritual.

Although the utterance of their ancient beliefs seems sometimes to establish contact with a tradition so deeply rooted that
centuries are momentarily abolished, and time has no meaning,
and the past is a long straight road that stretches out illimit-
ably, the end and origin of which is hidden only by the defective nature of the human eye; although old Poll, in her over-
grown backyard, all hollyhock seeds and drooping sunflowers
and cabbage-stalks, tugging at the front of her shapeless floral
dress to let in some air, surveying a white metallic sky and
warning that 'When the wind is in the east, 'Tis good for
neither man nor beast', and Ellen, looking fearfully at a solitary black crow perched on the clothes line and prophesying a
death before the week is out – although they seem sometimes
to have the power to transport me, their slightest more matter-
of-fact observations serving as magical incantations, to impossible and fabulous times, when even the wild flowers and birds

in Polebrook Woods had a profound and urgent significance for those who lived close to them, I know at the same
time that the people whose lives were shaped and governed by
these beliefs were impoverished and stultified by them. They
may have lived in harmony with their surroundings, but the
unquestioning assimilation of ideas effectively smothered the
development of any independent thought.

The family had no need of friends. In an intellectual sense
they found each other wholly satisfying and fulfilling, chiefly
because they all held the same opinions, and they zealously
upheld and confirmed each other in what were, alas, mostly
erroneous views on all conceivable subjects. They spoke in an
undifferentiated idiom, and the same words and phrases recurred so frequently in their discourse that it was sometimes
difficult to distinguish one from another, and when they all
assembled, as they did for weddings or funerals, their collective
conversation sounded like the dialogue of some badly-written
play which had failed to take any account of differences in
character. They shared a single conglomerate personality, not
only in the universally believed superstitions and prejudices,
but even in their personal characteristics. The men were expected to be selfish, aggressive and cruel, and any departure
from this was considered unmanly. The women were tradi-
tionally martyrised and self-effacing, and they submitted to
their husbands' bullying and unkindness as one submits to an
inclement season or a serious illness. The development of any
individual skills or abilities, the realization of distinctive attributes or qualities were not considered to be the purpose of
human life. They stood like fallow or uncultivated fields,
strangled by weeds and stones, choked by whatever by chance
found its way there.

They had begun to arrive in the town in the eighteen-sixties.
Until that time, those members of the family who were in the
shoe trade had walked the distance to Northampton two or
three times a week, to supply themselves with the leather
which they then carried back to the little workshops behind the
cottages, to cut into uppers or stitch into shoes. But Thomas

Timms was lazy. He would sit throughout the summer under the wooden latticework porch, while his last and awl lay unattended on the bench and mice made their nest in the waste leather that had accumulated on the red stone flags. When his wife remonstrated with him he would allege lameness or blindness ('I'm gooin' dark, woman'), or would cough and say pathetically that he hadn't many more years left to him. In spite of their harshness, nearly all of the men lived in a childish dependence upon their women, and they were unable to cope with real illness. It was always the women who hid the first symptoms of cancer or consumption, who concealed the emaciated arms and the blood-stained handkerchiefs, throwing themselves into their work with increased energy, as though the effect of routine everyday things would be to render their imminent collapse or death impossible. But the men had only to be afflicted with a sore throat for them to exact a constant, unflagging solicitude from their wives, and unless the women shared their own anxiety and preoccupation they were taxed with indifference and accused of 'wanting them out of the way'.

By 1861 Mary Timms knew that their future no longer lay in the parish where they had lived for so long. She knew that there was no longer any call for their ancient country skills – the ability to make wine from the dark, acrid stinging-nettles that grew in the ditches or to foretell the weather from the restlessness of the sheep in the fields, to cure warts by soaking them in urine, or to catch rooks and starlings for food, and, accordingly, she persuaded her husband to leave the great network of kinsfolk that lay like a huge cobweb halfway across the county, and to cease the ritual weekly visit to the churchyard where their dead lay. One October morning in 1861 they piled on a handcart half a dozen plain wooden chairs, a length of coconut matting, a picture of Christ driving the moneylenders from the temple and a bundle of household effects tied up in a coarse blanket, and they set out for Northampton on foot. Their material possessions were few, but with them they brought the remembrance of a long past, which was to reassure and comfort them in the alien world of the streets. They carried a wealth of ancient lore and dialect, embedded in everyday speech as the impress of a delicate fern may be retained for a thousand years in a seam of coal. For when they moved into the town their 'peasant' characteristics were not automatically surrendered with the change of environment as identity papers may be surrendered at the frontier of a new country.

The inherited traditions and beliefs lay untouched by compulsory education: at the most important moments of their lives they fell back upon some secret source within themselves, an underground river that nourished and watered their profoundest beliefs, and that ran on independently of official teachings, official religion, which always rested lightly and precariously as fragments of driftwood on the surface. Their attitudes to the natural world and to each other – the most powerful forces in their existence – were the residue of something of great antiquity, and could not be relinquished at the command of an imperious spinster with pince-nez, a pointed nose and a quarter-to-three walk. Until he died my great-grandfather refused to believe that the world was round. He did not trust the globe which his teachers had for six years assured him was a faithful representation of the planet on which he lived, or rather he did not trust the teachers, who so mysteriously sought to coax or bully him away from the truths imparted to him by his parents. His brother, who emigrated to Australia, in response to his anxious and insistent demands, wrote to inform him that during the journey to Australia the ship had not gone downhill but had appeared to remain on a level surface all the way. This irrefutable first-hand piece of evidence confirmed him for all time in his conviction of the earth's flatness. During the war he was heard telling one of his grandchildren that any contrary view he heard must have been propagated by the Germans in the hope of immobilizing the British fleet with fears of sudden escarpments and precipitous slopes if they ventured from harbour.

Not only did the change of environment not weaken traditional customs and ideas, it actually strengthened and intensified certain beliefs. Even today some of the family can still recite fragments of the Christmas Mummers' play, with its theme of death and resurrection, although it can't have been performed for more than a hundred years:

> In comes I, St George, a worthy knight,
> I'll spill my blood for England's right;
> Show me the man that bids me stand,
> I'll cut him down with my courageous hand.

They remembered the Mayday songs and the Plough Monday procession, and the raddled faces of the plough witches and the magic-making that ensured the fecundity of the earth for the coming season. Instead of yielding up their ancient knowledge in exchange for the superior wisdom of their educators, they sheltered it against what they regarded as an arbitrary assault upon some of their most cherished beliefs. Instead of abandoning the age-old prejudices, the superstitious mind transferred its fears to the trappings of the new industrial society, which were perhaps even more mysterious and incomprehensible than the phenomena of nature.

Ellen refused all her life to use a telephone. The only time it became unavoidable – she was called one day to the general store (a fateful and dreaded summons which everybody in the street feared) where she had to be informed of the death of a relative – she held the instrument at arm's length and shouted at the top of her voice, as though she believed that the instrument itself were the sole source of the misfortune it was transmitting. Whenever she wanted to watch the television a neighbour had to be called in to turn it on, although, it must be admitted, this did not prevent her from following at a respectful distance the vicissitudes of her favourite Western heroes. When she first acquired a gas-stove – a poor spindly blackened and second-hand contrivance – she showed her new possession proudly to her husband, who, instead of sharing her delight, flatly refused to partake of anything cooked inside it because of alleged poison in the gas. He ordered her to have it removed, but she stood firm, and had recourse to the perilous subterfuge of cooking his dinner every day in the gas-stove and transferring it to an open fire a few minutes before he was expected home from work – he was fortunately so punctual that neighbours said they could set their clocks by him. For eight years her action went undetected, and her husband did not complain. It was not until one very cold day when he had been sent home early that he caught her in the act of removing a pan of stew from the hated gas-stove. He threw the dinner at the wall in anger; not so much in protest against the slow and protracted poisoning he had suffered, but against the sustained success of his wife's deception. But the pretence did not stop there. It had to be maintained until the day he died. The meals were cooked by gas, but placed on the open fire before he came in. He must have known the truth, but he insisted upon a continuation of the ritual, possibly as a reprisal against the deceit, since he knew that this involved a good deal of unnecessary work for his wife.

A hot dry summer in the nineteen-fifties was attributed to the television aerials, which, it was claimed, were absorbing the moisture from the atmosphere, thereby preventing the usual precipitation from watering the earth. They were concerned and fretful the whole summer long, and their anxiety was only allayed by the abundant rainfall of the following autumn.

For a long time they were not happy in the town, and it needed several generations for them to become adjusted to the new surroundings. One Sunday dinner-time Edwin Youl came out of 'The Garibaldi' to find a big Daimler parked in the road. One of his companions offered him a pound to drive it to the bottom of the street and back. Boastful, like all our menfolk, he declared that there was nothing he couldn't do if he set his mind to it and spurred on by the doubts of his drinking companions, he drove away in the great car. The women, wearing their husbands' caps back to front as they always did indoors, came to the doorstep, and a loud cheer followed his advance down the street. It was not long before he lost control of the vehicle, having until that day never driven anything more powerful than a brewery dray. Seized by panic, he stood up in the driver's seat, clutching the windscreen, and bellowed at the top of his voice, 'Whoa, you bugger, whoa!'

The men all displayed this brash male confidence in their ability to do anything. It was considered another proof of their 'manliness'. They knew everything too, and never admitted themselves baffled or at a loss to explain anything. Before their women they would hold forth on every subject under the sun, although much of what they said was absurd and grotesque, and sometimes made complete nonsense, like Edwin Youl's solemn pontificating about the shape of the world.

'They used to have the right idea about criminals in the old days. Birch 'em till they bleed and then rub salt in the wounds.'

'The blacks only come to this country so as they can get round our women – they like our fresh clean English girls.'

'We was put here to behave ourselves lowly and reverently to our betters.'

In their opinions they were aggressive and dogmatic, possibly because somewhere they sensed the inadequacy of them, their lack of real information, their inability to give intelligible expression to their ideas, and if anyone assailed their views they had frequent and spontaneous recourse to violence. If Edwin Youl was sometimes found lying in the road it was not always because he had drunk too much, and might well have been because he had met someone with views as strong as his own and a heavier punch. They were not capable of abstract argument. Every opinion expressed was regarded as a fundamental characteristic of the person expressing it, a physical attribute like the colour of his hair or the shape of his nose (and perhaps in this they were not entirely wrong) and an attack upon opinions was the equivalent of a personal bodily assault, and the transition to physical force was a quick and logical process. In a family, if an argument developed from conflicting social and political views, it would not be long before husband and wife invoked each other's conjugal shortcomings, their ingratitude or laziness or drunkenness, and the discussion would end in tears and sullen silences and sulkings that often lasted for days.

There were many examples of fear and inability to cope with the devices and inventions of the new industrial society. Refusal to have gas or electricity in the house was quite common. Thomas Timms believed that the virility of men in whose houses electricity had been installed underwent a diminution – as if it were a rival, all the more powerful for being intangible. For many years Ellen would not allow herself to be photographed, protesting that no one wanted a picture of an old woman they could see every day, alleging that she had no time or had nothing fit to be seen in, in order to conceal her uneasiness about possible consequences of exposure to the camera's baleful eye. It was with great difficulty that she was persuaded to stand on the back doorstep one sunny afternoon, with her husband's protective arm around her shoulder, in her best apron and the black astrakhan hat that she was reputed to wear even when she went to the lavatory. The ceremony was attended by all the neighbours, who came to the garden wall and stood critically with their elbows cradled in their hands, or little finger crooked in the corner of the mouth with the rest of the hand splayed across the cheek – characteristic attitude of women on a million doorsteps, silent witnesses of paupers' funerals, evictions, street-quarrels, midnight departures, pregnant brides and rickety children.

They have always been suspicious of hospitals, workhouses, institutions and asylums, which loomed like a physical threat over the streets, buildings they never came to terms with. Hospitals are still places to die in. It is still believed that they 'use you', they cut you up, they experiment on you, they give you drugs never before administered to human beings. For twenty years Ellen kept an unworn elaborately embroidered nightgown locked away in a drawer 'just in case'. This meant in case of sudden illness and an unexpected removal to hospital. The only gesture she could make against the alien world that had the mysterious power to take possession of you and carry you off as soon as you became ill was to die with dignity. When at the age of eighty-seven she fell in the back garden and broke her thigh while knocking down plums from the tree with a line prop, her overriding worry was not the pain she felt, but the fact that somebody had produced an old darned calico nightie for her, and no one paid any attention to what were considered the ramblings of an old woman in pain about the special night-gown that had lain so long in the bottom drawer of the wardrobe, waiting ceremonially to adorn her death. Behind her agitation lay again a sense of inferiority of her own ways and her own life, the feeling of shame at even the things she wore.

The fear of buildings extended, and still does, to any public place – libraries, railway stations, cafés. At holiday time they would wander anxiously from platform to platform, putting repeated questions to everyone in sight about the destination of the train, retaining all the while a profound disbelief that any train could actually transport people like themselves to a place they actually wanted to arrive at. They felt there must be a catch in it somewhere. A bedraggled family group would wander dubiously from one café to another in wet seaside resorts, never summoning the courage to enter any of them, although they were all indistinguishable one from another. They would scrutinize identical menus and prices, and express doubts about the state of the kitchens, looking enviously at those securely installed inside enjoying their plaice and chips.

At length, after much deliberation, they would enter nervously, tentatively, as though afraid of being shown the door as soon as they set foot inside. They would sit down, oppressed and submissive, anxious about not being able to catch the eye of the waitress, displaying an exaggerated gratitude when she condescended to serve them, and not daring to venture beyond a fish tea with bread and butter and a pot of tea for four. When they had successfully ordered, the tension would be relaxed for a while, only to be renewed with the worry about eating properly. They would dab surreptitiously at the stream of soup that somehow contrived to escape from the unwonted shape of the spoon and trickle perversely down the chin, lick the corner of a handkerchief and wipe it round the stained mouth of a child, apologizing obsequiously to the waitresses for its unwillingness to eat all the batter that comprised the largest part of the meal, 'He's just the same at home, always has been', threatening it with a good hiding, not because they were really angry, but because they felt it necessary to placate the waitress, the limits of whose power in the confines of the café they had no way of assessing.

They were haunted by the perpetual fear of 'being shown up in public', by thoughtless children, outspoken relatives or unreliable husbands. They were profoundly ashamed of their way of living and were at great pains to conceal it from the outside world. They were like people who possessed some shameful characteristic – eunuchs or bald actresses – and whose life would have been ruined by its disclosure. Other people had to be prevented at all costs from gaining knowledge of their customs and habits, their thoughts and ideas. If anybody called unexpectedly at the house, an elaborate tidying-up operation would have to be performed before the intruder could be asked in – dirty overalls thrown behind the sofa, crumpled newspapers thrust under a cushion together with the darned and patched underwear drying by the fire, the dirty crockery removed from the table. While somebody opened the door the rest of the family craned their necks and listened anxiously to learn the purpose of this irruption into the secrecy of their lives, which were felt to be no less unworthy for being identical with everybody else's.

They had no notion of the conventions governing relationships with people like waiters or officials or shopkeepers, and they would alternate uneasily and jerkily between an attitude of surly truculence and defiance and an effusiveness that would lead them indiscriminately to pour out confidences to indifferent and embarrassed strangers. Away from familiar surroundings they were unable to cope. When it became necessary to travel they would lay in an exhaustive supply of all kinds of food, piles of sandwiches and cakes and fruit, as though they doubted the availability of wholesome and dependable nourishment in places they had never visited. Even on the shortest journeys, as soon as the bus or train had left behind the purlieus of the town, the flasks of tea and tomato sandwiches and bananas would make their appearance, consolatory bags of sweets, reassuring home-prepared foods. Even if the reason for the journey were a pleasant one – a holiday or works outing – the departure was likely to be onerous and rueful, attended by a complicated ritual of verifying that doors and windows were locked, gas-taps turned off, the electricity safe, and urging neighbours to keep an eye on the place, and ensuring that the parlour curtains were not drawn at an angle likely to encourage housebreakers or prying passers-by. Any prolonged absence from home infected several weeks before the actual departure with endlessly repeated instructions to those left behind, lachrymose leave-takings and doubts about the safety of the travellers. Even in the spring of 1965, before leaving on a dream-holiday-for-the-elderly, two aunts were shame-facedly surprised sewing five-pound notes into their corsets. Their reluctance to leave home was complemented by a profound distrust of all people in strange places, whose accent and manners and customs were alien and suspect. They were so ill-equipped to leave the familiar surroundings that a kins-woman who had not visited a sister for ten years, when charged with neglecting her nearest and dearest, burst into tears and admitted that she had not dared to face the three-hour journey on the slow and bumpy service bus that was the only available transport, because of her need to pay frequent visits to the lavatory, and the violence she feared would be done to her bladder if she risked a period of three hours denied access to a toilet.

But their exile and alienation was perhaps most apparent on rare occasions when they found their way into museums or art-galleries or theatres. Occasionally, on Bank Holidays, a vague consciousness that it might be 'good for the children' would impel them to make a solemn and respectful excursion to one of the local museums, and they would gaze with impregnable incuriosity at a penny-farthing bicycle or a *tenue de bal circa* 1840 or stuffed North American Feline Quadrupeds or squat glass cases full of faience and majolica and incense jars of the T'ang dynasty. If they were unable to create an immediate and spontaneous connection between the objects exhibited and their own lives they would display no interest in them. Everything had to stand in some relation to themselves, and they could not conceive of the independent existence of anything if it did not implicate and concern them in a personal way. They would gaze impassively at Ingres nudes and say, 'How would you like to wake up and see that on the other side of the bed every morning?', or they would finger the fabrics covering bustles and farthingales and wonder how people managed if

they were 'took short' in such elaborate and cumbrous cos-
tume, or they would survey cabinets full of Meissen or Spode
ware, and commiserate with the washers-up. Rarely, they
would stray into exhibitions of abstract painting or sculpture,
and this would involve too brusque and shocking a confronta-
tion with new and alien values: they became really angry,
convinced that they were the victims of a great swindle.

For until recent times they still retained a theoretical respect
for 'real art', which showed itself in treasured collections of
Zonophone recordings of arias from *Madame Butterfly* and
La Traviata, or in the ability to recite dramatic and portentous
fragments of poems about death laying its icy hand on kings
and roads winding uphill all the way. Their taste in these
things was merely the cultural counterpart of submission to the
social values of their betters, and as they freed themselves from
social dependence, so the cultural vassalage disappeared also,
and their not very substantial and vicarious contact with the
artistic and intellectual standards of their country was weakened still further. They visited music-halls and theatres, where
their most vociferous appreciation was extended to sketches
that ridiculed and disparaged ballet or opera or Shakespeare or
poetry. The loudest applause was always reserved for the reassurance they received of the worthlessness of those things
without which they managed so well. The jokes about opera
being something in which people get stabbed and instead of
bleeding sing, the caricature of the balcony scene from *Romeo
and Juliet* performed by North Country comedians spluttering
'art thous' and 'wherefores' in mock-posh accents, the bur-
lesque transvestite ballet, all served to emphasize their exclu-
sion from such things.

The anger at non-representational art was the anger of anyone brought abruptly face to face with ideas which he has no
use for, but which he finds form the very basis of somebody
else's philosophy. They did not admit it willingly that anything
exceeded their ability to understand, and in consequence violence had to be done to everything they encountered in order to
accommodate it. Art and music could be safely disregarded
because of their association with grotesque and impossible

people, with long hair, affected mannerisms and doubtful sexuality. Abstract art was a deception, a piece of trickery. Everything that occurred had to be reduced or adapted until it could
be contained within their restricted scheme of things, which
they did with the determination of a woman who refuses to
acknowledge her age and continues to force her recalcitrant
flesh into bodices of steel and whalebone.

One day Ellen was taken to the National Gallery. I remember her look of bewilderment and the anxiously reiterated
question, 'Well, what's it all for?' Nothing but the question
why. Our Gran and the High Renaissance. She stood for a
quarter of an hour looking up at the great canvases as if she
expected the works of art in some miraculous ways to descend
from their positions on the wall and to yield up personally
their secret splendour to the old woman from Green Street,
Northampton, in her astrakhan hat and elastic-sided boots.
They looked at each other uncomprehendingly, the world's
masterpieces and our Gran, and neither budged an inch. She
went away, baffled and disappointed, confirmed in the suspicion that she had been abused.

Not long after this expedition the patient and perplexed
Ellen was persuaded to attend a performance of *Othello*. She
sat silently if disapprovingly through most of the play, but
towards the end, when Othello, doubting his wife's faithful-
ness, responds scathingly to her protestations of innocence,
Ellen could not resist offering the wronged woman some advice, and in a crowded and silent auditorium a passionate
voice was raised above those of the players on the stage, 'Goo
on, me duck, slosh him one!' Spontaneous and instinctive in
all her reactions, she could not be expected to appreciate
dramatic conventions or tragic necessity, and was only irri-
tated by the artifice and contrivance demanded by the theatre.
Perhaps life afforded her enough examples of dramatic experience and conflict without her feeling any need to supplement it
with theatre. For her it was perhaps an unnecessary luxury, an
incomprehensible refinement. She was able to understand
things only in terms of her own life and experience.

3. Neighbours

In the streets themselves immediate and spontaneous relationships sprang up between neighbours, and most people were on terms of intimacy with those around them. There was little sense of selectivity in the choice of friends, little sense of seeking out the company of one particular person rather than another. To do so would have been to incur suspicion of clandestine or improper relationships – the only conceivable reason for such furtive and unnecessary exertions in view of the circle of kinsfolk extensive enough to people a dozen lifetimes. The closest links were generally established with immediate neighbours. Those a few doors distant were treated with cordiality which diminished progressively as their dwelling-place became farther removed, until those at the end of the street had to be content with a cursory nod and the briefest glance of recognition. Physical propinquity governed the warmth of feeling extended to the neighbours. Only the fancy-women and the few men who habitually refused to work were under the necessity of actively seeking out their companions – they were shunned by most people. The only quality demanded of others was 'neighbourliness', a rather vague and indefinable attribute. It suggested someone who could be relied upon to be present at times of great affliction and suffering, but who took good care to keep at a distance so long as the family, self-contained and self-sufficient, went about its daily business. In this way it was possible for Aunt Mary Ann to lie unconscious at the bottom of her steep flight of cellar steps for nearly two days before it was realized that anything was wrong. It was not that people were not interested in the comings and goings of their neighbours. On the contrary, a detailed knowledge of their every movement was of major importance, provided that the acquisition of such knowledge did not entail personal involvement. If Aunt Mary Ann had been well she would have considered an intrusion into her home, even by someone anxious about her welfare, an intolerable affront.

No one minded attending to the small material needs of the old-age pensioner who had lived in the street all her life, or of the woman lying-in, but the madwoman and the permanent invalid were sedulously avoided. It was less a lack of charity than a fear of 'getting too thick with people', a fear which pervaded all their dealings with each other. If you committed this indiscretion, you would be caught up in a network of involved and demanding relationships from which you might never again be able to extricate yourself. Other people were sure to abuse your hospitality, take advantage of your kindness and exploit your generous nature. It was as if they were all conspiring your downfall in collusion and secrecy, and were only waiting for you to make yourself known to them so that you would expose yourself to their malice, just as witches were formerly believed to lie in wait for locks of hair to fall into their possession, or nail-parings of people against whom they wanted to work charms. The family sought to contract no bonds, no obligations, no relationships beyond those exacted by duty. They seemed to believe that revelation of the self to another human being in some way undermined or debilitated the personality. For this reason they fortified and guarded themselves like a beleaguered town against the encroachments of others, into whose power they might fall should they be careless enough to part with the smallest fragment of their being. 'Not to be beholden to anybody' was the chief aim of their existence, and it is this that even now forbids some of the oldest and neediest members of the family to draw the old-age pension to which they are entitled. It is not that they object to the principle of state pensions for doctrinaire reasons. They simply fear that if they accept the allowance some secret and undisclosed obligation may later be made known, some unacceptable condition come to light.

The only way to avoid the onslaughts and intrusions of others was to keep yourself uncompromisingly to yourself. When it became clear that Ellen was dying, she was taken home from the hospital at her own request, and a constant stream of neighbours called to see her, none of whom succeeded in advancing beyond the threshold. She was convinced that they could not be calling out of solicitude, but at best out of curiosity, and at worst to come poking their noses into her scant belongings, to see what she'd got that was worth taking as soon as her eyes were closed.

Similarly, Ellen would never believe herself possessed of qualities that could cause others to single her out for her own sake. When Mrs V. claimed to be moved by Ellen's kindliness and the affection she bore her family, and invited her repeatedly into her back kitchen, Ellen was embarrassed and suspicious. Discreet inquiries revealed that she had already made overtures to many of the neighbours in turn (which had, of course, met with summary rebuttal), and it was generally agreed that she was a strange woman whom it would be better to avoid. When she committed suicide any guilt the street may have felt was allayed by the reassuring decision of the coroner that she had taken her life while the balance of her mind was disturbed. It released them from any suspicion that they might have been able to forestall her last desperate act.

Because the relationships between neighbours were so arbitrarily established they were fragile and easily disrupted. They were based upon observance of a rigid and complex system of rules and conventions, any infringement of which could abruptly transform the closest friendships into violent implacable enmity. People who had lived in harmony for twenty years could throw the whole street into disarray because of a betrayed confidence, too much curiosity or misplaced criticism of a neighbour's behaviour.

Children were the commonest source of discord. Two women in the street lived together, ostensibly as sisters, but their neighbour's child – a girl of ten – was heard to assert that they were really mother and daughter, and claimed to be sisters only so that the elder might walk abroad dressed up like a dog's dinner and avoid the obloquy which such behaviour, attended by a general awareness of her true age, would inevitably call forth. This was duly reported to the alleged mother and daughter, who reasoned that a child of ten would be unlikely to arrive independently at such a conclusion, and traced the source of the calumny without much difficulty to the child's mother. The two women burst unceremoniously into the house next door – an unthinkable step under normal circumstances – and gave the indiscreet neighbour a good hiding in her own kitchen.

Certain subjects could never be broached between neighbours. Sex and money could be alluded to only in the most general terms, and although a series of sex crimes might have everybody in agreement about the urgent need for public whippings and beatings as adequate punishment for such enormities, and the rising cost of living was a constant starting point for a bout of mutual commiseration, to introduce these subjects in any personal connection was absolutely forbidden. Of the two most violent street quarrels in memory, one had begun with a neighbour seeking to borrow money for luxury goods which she had secretly obtained 'on strap', and the other with a careless remark about the bedsprings not having creaked for a year or two in one household. People's trust and allegiance could be withdrawn at a minute's notice, as if they were something tangible, a scrap of paper certifying that someone was qualified to drive a motor car or entitled to own a dog. People's relationships with each other were completely gratuitous, and they never seemed to evolve because of any innate qualities which any of the participants may have possessed. The rôle of friend and neighbour was completely passive, the sympathetic though supine recipient of domestic woes, family troubles and marital discord. They could be as featureless as a confidant in classical tragedy. Anybody would do as a friend and comforter. They simply had to be there. No one sought love or understanding, and even less did they seek ideas. It was assumed that everybody voted Labour, didn't have much money and knew the difference between right and wrong, and only if you went out of your way to proclaim any divergent view would you be treated accordingly, like the Misses Hands or Mrs Hitchcock, whose standoffish demeanour soon earned her the sobriquet 'Old Mother Scratch-arse'.

Lily and Bessie Hands had come down in the world. Their father was said to have owned a small boot factory, long since absorbed by a larger firm, and he was presumed to have 'drunk away all his profits'. The two sisters crammed the narrow front parlour with moth-eaten Sheraton chairs and drank only from cracked Spode chinaware, shielded from the dust and noise of the street and the bad words chalked on the pavement only by a length of dusty gauze curtain. For nearly forty years they guarded intact a life brought into the street from a very different milieu. There emanated from their person something alien and exotic, discernible in the oddly gracious lifting of a hand in acknowledgement of a salutation, a scent of lavender, black straw hats and parasols and cambric handkerchiefs. Having no contact with the changing fashions of their own social group, they retained for a lifetime those of their own youth. They worshipped God, voted Conservative and spoke to no one but each other. I was the only person in the street whose existence they acknowledged, possibly because I was unaccountably 'ever so well spoken' at an early age. Finally Lily, who was much older than her sister, was taken to hospital, where she remained for some weeks before dying of cancer. Bessie, with a worried look on her sad cadaverous face, said she had no intention of leaving her sister in a place like that, where all kinds of students and coloureds had been Messing her About. 'My sister and I,' she said with dignity, 'are going back to our Maker the same as we left our mother.'

Although they took no part in its life, over the years the Misses Hands were gradually absorbed and accepted by the street. But nobody else failed so flagrantly to conform. Everybody was anxious to show that he deferred absolutely to the prevailing values. Not only was there almost complete uniformity in the appearance of each house – the flaking brown painted exterior was characteristic, with a potted plant in the window in its great crinkly green or pink china pot, or painted Alsatian dog, or coy little girl tugging at the bottom of her plaster skirts – but inside each house life tended to follow a similar pattern.

There was the same back room with the high old-fashioned blackleaded grate, the faded blue velvet curtain screening the stairs and the washing strung from wall to wall, while the old man sat in the zinc bathtub scrubbing his back with a coarse loofah and with only a clothes horse for modesty, the children pored over *Lord Snooty and his pals* on the threadbare carpet and Gran dozed in a corner, eating her Old-Fashioned Winter Mixture and intermittently knitting a kettle-holder, only rousing herself from sleep to place an occasional sententious and irrelevant proverb.

Everybody felt constrained to make his life appear identical with everybody else's. There was no differentiation in the way people spoke, in their ideas and beliefs and attitudes, whether it was the communal prejudice about the blacks or the Jews passed to and fro in the Public Bar of 'The Garibaldi' of an evening like the single eye and tooth of the Graeae, or the petrified wisdom that fell like pebbles from the mouths of the women as they gathered every morning outside the general store. Their conversation consisted of identical expressions and idioms, and even the voice inflexions did not vary as they talked in the same sepulchral way about the death of a neighbour or the rise in price of some indispensable commodity, as if both of these phenomena had a shared and equally incomprehensible origin. The women always appeared downtrodden and oppressed, and as they spoke disaster always appeared imminent, death, privation and want lay permanently in wait.

It was strange that our family, or indeed any other, should be so jealous of its identity, when it showed so little deviation from the pattern of the lives of other people in the street. Perhaps it was the awareness that nothing distinguished them but the family of which they formed part that made them vaunt their uniqueness and transmit the idea of a vague superiority to their children. The aloofness which we were taught earned us nobody's affection, and our children were often lonely and friendless. When they escaped from the tight mesh of kinship, which they sometimes did, like rabbits breaking loose from a snare, they were made to feel that they had done something unbecoming and discreditable. As children

grew older and became wilful and refractory, it was insisted
that such characteristics must have been acquired from other
people.

When it came to marriage there was a process of selection –
or perhaps it was really an elimination – like that which determined the choice of friends or neighbours. There was the
same arbitrary system in the final and (for them) irrevocable
decision of choosing a husband or wife, and his or her availability seemed to be the major determining factor in the choice.
Most of the couples in the street had met either in the neighbourhood or at their place of work, and the suitability of a
match, the compatibility of two people, would have seemed to
them irrelevant luxuries not worthy of serious attention. It was
not surprising, therefore, that disillusionment with marriage
began early. In the home the men became taciturn and resentful, and often gave way to outbursts of gratuitous violence.
They always regarded the children as no concern of theirs, and
often drove them to seek refuge with the gentler downtrodden
mother, with her helpless petulant voice and protective arms
warding off the blows that her husband would sometimes ad-
minister indiscriminately in his drunkenness. This violence
would alternate with periods of boozy sentimentality, and the
children learned early in life that there was likely to be little
reciprocation in their relationships, when the same action was
capable of evoking a different response every time, depending
entirely upon capricious and inexplicable changes of mood on
the part of the parents. They were not capable of dealing with
each other emotionally as well as socially and, as the years
went by, the outward sameness of each household often
masked the bitterest strife and suffering, which were denied an
outlet by the suspicion and pride that made its members regard
all outsiders as potential enemies or evil-wishers. Their personality remained undeveloped, their intelligence often unrealized
beneath the uniformity, and their lives turned inwards to the
family, sometimes mistakenly seeking there the cause of their
bewilderment and frustration, which never disturbed the surface homogeneity of the street.

All my mother's generation met their husbands or wives

either in the street or at the place of work, the only exception being Daisy, whose first encounter with her husband was generally disapproved of, considered exotic and *recherché*. This meeting had occurred on a day trip to Blackpool. The train was just pulling out of the station for the return journey when Daisy appeared on the platform at the last moment, breathless and dishevelled. The young cattle-drover from Brington extended a brawny arm and hauled her safely on to the moving train, a romantic gesture for which Daisy's sisters said he was to pay dearly in later years. Some of them even claimed that if he had been able to foresee his future life, not only would he have forborne from offering her his hand that day, but have given her a damn good shove instead in front of the train. It was the idea of travelling so far afield on such a simple errand as finding a husband that was viewed with disapprobation, when most of them had found partners with such remarkable facility. Distant excursions for such a purpose were highly suspect, the most charitable assumption being that she was 'too high in the instep', and thought that local boys weren't good enough for her, and the least charitable but most widespread that 'there was something the matter with her', something that prevented her from meeting a man like everybody else. The conditions for an acceptable husband were easily fulfilled, and, once again, they were not concerned so much with personal qualities as with his disponibility, his lack of obvious defects. Most of them knew what married life would mean for them anyway, and their parents represented a faithful image of their probable future. The frequent incidence of shotgun weddings often relieved them of any embarrassment of choice.

Whenever anyone was unhappy as the result of an unsuccessful relationship, they would cite the proverbs, 'There's more fish in the sea than ever came out of it' or 'He's not the only pebble on the beach', and, unlike most of their received wisdom, it was clear that they really meant it: for them all potential husbands or lovers were as lacking in the distinctive features as shingle on the beach or fish in a net, writhing in an undifferentiated silvery mass. People were all very much the same for them, and no human being was indispensable. It is difficult to know whether this attitude was deliberately acquired – premature death so frequently retrenched their relationships that they may have been forced to learn to exist without each other – or whether it was simply that they had never possessed the skill for profound and enduring relationships. Whatever the reason, it is certain that broken hearts and deep sorrows resulting from unhappy love-affairs did not occur. Fights and quarrels over disputed women were commonplace, but these developed more from wounded pride or a sense of proprietorship than from grief. They were often staged for the benefit of the public, seldom a means of assuaging any feeling of loss.

Once they had made their arbitrary choice they would always abide by it. 'As you make your bed, so you lay on it.' And they would frequently extract a perverse and bitter pleasure from their resignation to a lifetime's unhappiness. This stoical acceptance entitled them to the consolatory satisfaction of the most uncharitable judgements upon all people whose conduct differed in any way from their own. Although the practice of 'lowbelling' had ceased (a means of expressing public censure against anyone guilty of a breach of moral law, and which involved the assemblage of the whole neighbourhood before the house of the wrongdoer, adulterer or seducer, and the rattling of tins and kettles in disapproval), they nevertheless retained a variety of equally unequivocal if less clamorous methods of rebuke – oblique opprobrious remarks when they passed the offending party in the street, or anonymous letters that informed the miscreant that he or she was not fit to live among 'decent people'.

In the next street lived the Nancy Browns, who claimed to be brothers. No one questioned their relationship for many years, until one woman from a neighbouring street claimed to have known 'both their families'. On this tenuous piece of evidence – and she was a notorious troublemaker – attitudes changed abruptly. All the mothers in the street acquired a sudden retrospective insight into the depravity of the two men, remembered a smell of scent as they had passed them by, or 'something funny about the eyes' (always a sure way of recognizing sexual irregularity). Children were forbidden to play anywhere near the house for fear of their being defiled by the very presence of the Nancy Browns, and somebody recalled, or thought she recalled, having seen them offer sweets to children on the doorstep, liquorice allsorts or dolly mixtures polluted by the aberration of the two soft-spoken and inoffensive, epicene creatures who had offered them, and who had now been revealed in their true colours. Their appearance, it had to be admitted, belied their terrible vice. They were both of mild and asexual aspect, and both close upon sixty. Their age, together with the fact that they had deceived everyone for so long, only exacerbated the anger of the street. The women were more venomous than the men, and as well as the customary batch of anonymous letters, some of them devised more novel manifestations of disapproval, felt to be more in keeping with the particular case. One of the most respected women in the street took to assuming a walk and gestures of extreme lewdness whenever she met by chance one of the Nancy Browns in the fish-shop or in the cobbled jitty between two houses, a grotesque parody of sexual invitation, which never failed to amuse everybody in sight, to the great embarrassment and discomfiture of the Nancy Browns. All that was left for them was to move to another neighbourhood, which they accordingly did.

Many of those who lived in the streets professed great worldliness. They would be anxious for others to know that they were familiar with the phenomenon of homosexuality or prostitution, but it was basically superstition and ignorance which controlled their attitudes to such things. Indeed, the most usual reason for unrelenting ostracism was evidence of any form of sexual abnormality. Mrs B.'s predilection for young boys caused her a good deal of social embarrassment. She encouraged her teenage daughter to take home her boyfriends, to what end everybody knew. One foggy evening a boy from the Grammar School was on his way home when her front door opened and she called, 'I'm in a bit o' trouble, me duck, could you step inside a minute?' This the youth obligingly did, to be confronted, it was said, by Mrs B. quite naked.

(Why the detail of his being specifically a Grammar School boy should be remembered is uncertain – it seemed somehow to heighten the sense of his innocence and defencelessness.) Fortunately, Mrs B.'s husband, who had finished work early because of the fog, arrived just in time to prevent any further outrage against the boy and any further indiscretion on the part of his wife. He was said to have paid sums of money, varying in the neighbours' accounts of the incident from five to thirty pounds, in order to hush it up. The exact amount which had to be paid for the high principles of the injured child's parents to be temporarily set aside is unknown, but it was enough to fit out the entire house with new curtains as well as to acquire an ostentatious display of wax tulips for the front parlour window.

But the Nancy Browns and Mrs B.s were rare, and they only threw into relief the extreme outward orthodoxy of the rest. Most of the others were busy resigning themselves to a cheerless and completely predictable future: for the women passive submission to their husbands, and childbearing as frequent and unwelcome as an annual attack of influenza (in fact it became a casual and automatic process for them; Ellen used to tell that one day she had gone home feeling unwell, had gone to bed and had woken up in the night to find herself in labour, without having had any fore-warning of pregnancy); for the men a mechanical and joyless repetition of the sexual act, devoid of tenderness and imagination, a prolonged and wearisome piece of self-indulgence, like children eating sweets until they are sick, until one day, to their surprise, they go home to find that their wife 'has done her bottom button up for good'. Sexual activity was expected to cease in the early forties, and any sign of affection or physical attraction persisting beyond this age was considered unnatural and obscene. A great-aunt once confided to my mother that her husband was subject to terrible moods, 'just because he's still – what's the word? – virile, and of course I won't have anything to do with him that way. Sometimes on Sat'day night when he gets a drop o' beer inside him, he gets all happy' (a surprisingly delicate euphemism for them) 'and I tell him he's a dirty ole b., a man of his age acting like that.' She was as angry and resentful as she would have been if her husband had betrayed signs of some unexpected perversion in his sixtieth year.

Sex was always something furtive and shameful. The convention was that it didn't happen, and this pretence permitted them to be censorious or amused, according to their mood, at the expense of those who were indiscreet enough to give any intimation that it did. Mrs T. was a big woman, with a prodigious sexual appetite. Her next-door neighbour held the Snug of 'The Garibaldi' spellbound on Saturday nights with accounts of her sexual extravagances. When this wonder first came to live next door to her she had frequently been wakened in the night by what sounded like a death-rattle, and she had almost called in the doctor and the undertakers before she realized her mistake. Furthermore, the woman was reputed to be so strong that she could 'keep it in even against her husband's will, till he cried out for mercy and begged to be released'. And the old women would simulate shock and incredulity, and ask to be told all over again. They would never admit that sex concerned them in a personal way, and they only mentioned it obliquely and allusively to emphasize their own non-involvement. The women never admitted that it gave them pleasure. They would sometimes pretend to be amused by their husbands' agitation in anything so insignificant, but they gave to understand that they themselves remained immovable and impassive as granite cliffs assailed by the tide.

The attitude of the street towards its neighbours was compounded of mistrust and sympathy. 'Keep yourself to yourself, but let us know if you're in need.' Material need that is. It would be no good coming to us and telling us that you were entertaining an illicit passion or anything like that. We'd damn soon send you packing with platitudinous bits of advice about pulling yourself together and the wages of sin.

Whether the 'neighbourliness' of the streets, which reserved its manifestations for times of suffering or hardship, was the result of a genuine compassion or simply a kind of insurance against the time when the rôles of good neighbour and sufferer might be reversed, it is difficult to assess. One thing is certain.

There was very little of the warmth and comradeship which have come to be associated with life in working-class streets. It needed a death to occur before the neighbours stepped in, collected for wreaths and comforted the bereaved. A steady procession would then pay ceremonial visits to the dead, and the children would be made to touch the corpse so that they should not dream about what they had seen, and relatives would watch to see 'the bloom come back to the cheeks' which was believed to happen twenty-four hours after death. A black board would be nailed across the front window, and on the day of the funeral all the curtains in the street would be drawn, the children called in from play, and a great silence would descend.

And yet, even if it is true that in these ceremonies they achieved a certain dignity and sense of compassion, it is equally true that for most of the time Margie was disregarded as she stood on the doorstep talking about the devils in her head, and Edwin Youl could knock his children over the stones as much as he chose without a single voice being raised in public protest anywhere in the street. The ceremonial, the sympathy, were a kind of exorcism, were of a piece with the philosophy that urged them to 'look around at other people's troubles and see what a lot you've got to be thankful for', the idea that sufferings worse than your own should be a comfort to you, and indeed, only really existed for that purpose. If a sick child complained of pain, its mother would tell it to think of all the little children who were in hospital or who were blind, not intending that the child should dwell upon them to such an extent as to become sincerely afflicted by their plight, but simply as a salutary exercise to distract them from their own misfortunes. Dopey Freda, with her great uncontrolled eyes, who ran up and down the street grunting like a pig, was used by all the mothers in the neighbourhood as a threat and a warning. 'Don't pull them faces at me, you'll end up like Freda else if the wind changes.' 'Eat your dinner or you'll turn out dibby as Freda.' 'Behave yourself or I'll send you to live with Freda.'

There was much insensitivity and lack of imagination in rela-

tion to other people's unhappiness. When they heard of a disaster somewhere they went through the motions of being
affected by it – 'I see there's been another earthquake in South
America, shocking thing, ennit?' or 'I see that ole gal in
Bouverie Street's done away with herself, terrible yis', and then
in the next breath 'Did you back any winners?' or 'I got a nice
bit of ham at the Co-op.' Their sympathy was a perfunctory
piece of ritual, like touching wood, intended to ward off such
things from themselves. When someone died in the street
everybody came forward with offers of help. It was felt that by
taking part in a grief not your own you somehow managed to
forestall the next misfortune in your own life. By anticipating
the next tragedy you paid off a share of the suffering to come,
and this would mitigate the full force of the catastrophe when
it arrived.

As the coins dropped into the bowl of the woman collecting
for a wreath she was fulfilling some deep atavistic need to
placate the mysterious source of evil and suffering. She had a
glimpse too of her own body lying unattended in the cold front
parlour, the posthumous shame of meagre floral tributes, two
wreaths and a spray on her grave proclaiming the poverty of
her human relationships, and no one to sing her praises
when the old women gathered outside the corner shop. They
were afraid that their fundamental insecurity and isolation,
which in life they were able to conceal beneath the indifference
and self-sufficiency (what they called their 'pride'), might become apparent to all in death. They feared the ignominy of
being stranded in death, like Maud Holford who died on the
lav with eightpence in her purse and not enough furniture in
the house to pay for the burial, the horror of dying between
tiled walls with no familiar hands to bind up their hair in its
thin grey night-time plait, and no one to seek out the best night-
dress from its brown-paper bag in the landing cupboard, the
disgrace of the bare deal coffin without handles being jolted
through the streets on an unadorned hearse. . . .

They could commiserate at funerals and exchange a half-
amused word with Dopey Freda on their way to work, but
they couldn't help the children of Edwin Youl in the single

sagging bed which they had to share one night with their brother Joe's fancy-woman, who left behind her a mysterious illness called 'the itch' and a scent of Devon violets that clung to the children's calico shimmy with its lice pouring out of the bunched material at the neck whenever it was taken off. There was no comfort for the woman whose three sons were killed on the Somme and who stood on the doorstep for ten years calling to her dead boys among the children playing in the gutter, no sympathy for Doug Turner who married eighteen-stone May Tee and who was found on his wedding day astride on one of the painted wooden horses of the fair. And the streets were not alive with warmth and friendliness and soli-darity. Pride, fear and mistrust of other people inhibited their relationships, and denied them insight and compassion where it was often most needed. And their lives were not enriched, but became circumscribed and introspective.

Next door to us in Green Street lived Mrs Hawkes. Unlike most people we knew, she was at liberty to walk in and out of the house as she chose – a privilege extended to her only be-cause we were confident that she would never take advantage of it. She had access to the hiding-place of the front-door key, which hung from a string just inside the letterbox (as it did in almost every house in the street). At times of illness she would run in with egg-custards and pieces of pig-lard covered with a lead powder which she called 'the precipitate', and which was a cure for all aches and pains. (When she finally died of lung cancer, advanced to such a degree that the poison exploded through her skin in great viscous bubbles on the breast, she was found to have covered herself with the ointment which she claimed had never failed her.) In return for her ministrations all she sought was a sympathetic ear for her tale of woe, which she delivered as often as she could, like an actress who has once triumphed in a single rôle, and who seizes every oppor-tunity to recapture her brief moment of success and acclaim.

It was a familiar story, a son grown too big for his boots, a wife who thought she was the cat's whiskers, when, as Mrs Hawkes never ceased to affirm, she wasn't even the cat's arse. She expected no response to her lament. All she needed was to give way occasionally to the purgative effect of complaint and tears, and after she had delivered her monologue she would go away singing 'We'll gather lilocks in the spring again'. She and her daughter-in-law Iris were the last survivors of a long family quarrel which had begun when Iris's mother had ostentatiously presented her daughter and son-in-law her own house in Queen's Park Parade, a sombre villa with a bay window and stained-glass windows of Scenes from the Parables, a blue-and-red-tiled forecourt and three sooty fuchsias.

At the time of the union Iris's mother had visited Mr and Mrs Hawkes in Green Street. She had perched awkwardly on the edge of the old leather sofa in the parlour, hemmed and hawed and cast disparaging glances at the furniture. Finally, she had asked them point-blank what they intended giving Reg towards setting up home in the superior residential district to which he was being so graciously admitted. Mrs Hawkes said she hadn't given it much thought, but her husband had drawn himself up and said he didn't consider it his duty to provide his son with anything, and he had held up his ten fingers and said, 'As long as he's got these and as long as he's not afraid to use them no woman has anything to worry about.'

Iris's mother had said she'd gathered he was a bit tight-fisted, but she was flabbergasted to have found he was such a stingy old Jew. She would do everything in her power, fair means or foul, to prevent her daughter from marrying into such riff-raff, because her daughter had been brought up in the lap of luxury, and was even connected with some titled people on her father's side. (It was astonishing how many people in the streets claimed kinship with members of the aristocracy, or asserted that their forbears had been 'a real lady' or 'a gentleman by birth' or had 'owned houses'.) But the wedding had taken place, and, in order to be revenged, Iris's mother had attached strings to the gift of the house. They were to have it only on condition that Reg should renounce his family. 'Such small people', Iris's mother called them, 'such pathetically small people'. Reg had been only too willing to accede to his mother-in-law's demands. His parents had forced him to leave school at fourteen and to accept employment in a boot factory, although they knew this was repugnant to him, and it had been on his own initiative that he'd studied and bettered himself, gone to the Borough Treasurer's and got himself a worthwhile job, and then met a girl like Iris.

After the wedding all intercourse between the two families had ceased. Two or three times a year Reg would arrive unaccompanied in Green Street. With great display he would set down a jar of honey or a quarter of tea and a couple of past issues of *Woman's Own*, and would say, 'I've brought you a little physical and spiritual sustenance,' and his mother would tell him not to be so damn silly. As he walked away down the street, meticulously avoiding the dejecta on the pavement, he would vouchsafe me a smile of connivance, because, I imagine, I was reputed to be 'doing ever so well at the Grammar', and would therefore probably be expected to understand these things.

Two or three years later Iris's mother died, and on the day of the funeral Mrs Hawkes sat dressed in black, confident that the funeral car would call for her. Nobody came, and the feeling that they were so ashamed of her that she couldn't be trusted to behave herself and 'do things properly', even at a funeral, embittered the relationship still further. Not long afterwards Mr Hawkes died, and once the two chief protagonists were gone any lingering hope of a *rapprochement* between the two factions faded. Both Mrs Hawkes and her daughter-in-law felt they had a duty to their dead in sustaining the quarrel, and neither made any movement towards a reconciliation. Mrs Hawkes, as the older, declared that it was not for her to abase herself, while Iris claimed that since Mr Hawkes had initiated the rupture it was his widow's duty to make conciliatory overtures. They resolved to wait for death to vindicate them, as humble litigants might wait a lifetime for a tribunal to pronounce one way or the other upon the ownership of a cow or the boundary of a piece of land.

Mrs Hawkes' tale of woe did not change over twenty years. Incidental detail came and went, but the account of her martyrdom and misery remained substantially the same. It culminated in the day when her own granddaughter passed her by in the street without recognizing her. The same words, the same turns of phrase recurred at every recital. She seemed not to recall whether the person she was addressing had heard it before, or perhaps she thought it sufficiently interesting in its own right to bear unlimited repetition. Not that there was anything unusual in this. Most people's conversation was a soliloquy interrupted only by the fragmented soliloquy of the person with whom they were talking. They returned unceasingly to their own preoccupations. They only spoke to others as those burdened with guilt or the consciousness of some crime are sometimes said to find relief in confiding their secret to a deep well, or in shouting it aloud to empty fields – just as Midas whispered his shame to the reeds.

When we moved from the street we did not see Mrs Hawkes for eight years. I thought that enough shared experience bound us to her – for she had been good to us – to allow the relationship to continue, to warrant the journey of no more than a quarter of a mile at least occasionally. But on the day we moved she waved to the furniture van as it turned the corner, with the desolation of one waving to kinsfolk on an Atlantic liner steaming out of Southampton. Her leavetaking was tearful and final. She knew that it was not in our scheme of things to retain contact with people who were not related to us when we no longer lived next door to them, or were at least not thrown together with them in the most exceptional circumstances – in wartime or seaside boarding-houses. Mrs Hawkes went out of our lives without any kind of fuss. She had entered them because she had chanced to be there, and she left because we moved half a dozen streets away to take up a similar relationship with whomsoever we might find there. A Christmas card was exchanged for about three years, with a vague scribbled message in indelible pencil about coming up for a cup of tea one day, and then, as by some mutual telepathic consent, even that stopped. When we left her there was no need to prolong the simulated friendship; the feigned interest in her life could cease.

It was not until many years later that we met her again by chance in the street. Immediately the threads were taken up

again, as if we had left her the day before, and the lament on
filial ingratitude was resumed as if it had never been interrupted. Nothing had happened in eight years to dull the pain
of the insults she had suffered, and she told of the same events
– the funeral of Iris's mother, and the granddaughter who
didn't know her – with a bitterness and acrimony that had not
diminished. Or perhaps it was simply that the sight of us reminded her of that period of her life, and she could find no
other way of reconstituting the relationship that had existed
than by rehearsing the sorrows of eight years previously. The
new neighbours were apparently not interested, people no
longer had time to share the troubles of an old woman alone in
the world. (Neither had we. She didn't know that we had listened to her just to the point where we felt we might legiti-
mately be able to claim her help in return some day. Our in-
dulgence had been designed to place her under obligation to us,
and when we were in trouble we would arrive like creditors at
her door to exact the precise amount of sympathy or assistance
due to us.) She said the street hadn't been the same since we
left. She had taken in an egg-custard to the little girl when she
had had measles, but she had turned up her nose at it and said
it looked like sick. On parting we made no arrangements to see
her again, and a few months later she died. We were scandal-
ised because Reg had been two-faced enough to insert an
obituary notice in the local paper: 'In memory of a devoted
mother. Asleep in God's beautiful garden.'

Most of the relationships in the street were tacit and mutually convenient bargains, quite empty of real feeling. The family was the only important unit. Although there may have been
a good deal of surface bonhomie, cups of tea and gossip over
the garden wall, the dialogues between bald Amy and Mr Wil-
cox through the wall of their adjoining lavatories as they each
sat with the *News of the World* on Sunday afternoons, no one
pretended that other people really mattered.

On the night when Freda was heard screaming in the jitty
no one paid any attention. I don't know whether they all
closed the windows as we did, and drew the curtains and said
what a terrible thing it was to be afflicted like that and please

God may it never touch any of us. Freda was found by her mother some hours later with her dress torn to shreds and her mouth bleeding. Some young men on their way home had found her wandering in the jitty in her nightwear, and had taken it in turns to enjoy the novelty of sexual knowledge of a thirty-five-year-old half-witted virgin. Of course the next day the street was appalled by what had happened, by what many of them had heard happening. It appeared that her mother had put her to bed, and when she had assured herself that she was asleep, she'd crept out to 'The Garibaldi' for a Guinness. Freda, waking up and finding herself alone, perhaps for the first time in her life, had gone out in search of the absent mother. 'And there she sat,' said the neighbours, 'boozing as if she didn't have a care in the world'. They were not slow to suggest suitable and savage punishments for such a terrible crime, but their passion and fervour were only a kind of excuse, a mask for their own indifference and their failure to intervene when they were needed.

Other people were only interested in so far as a knowledge of the things that happened to them enhanced our own lives: we arrogated to ourselves their loves and crimes and deaths with undissembled rapacity, aware that so long as we were the only possessors of such knowledge we would be sought after by everyone in the street. The woman who had found the suicide was fêted like a national heroine, the one who was first to learn of the dubious colour of Mrs D.'s baby – muffled up in so many covers and shawls that no one saw it for the first three months – how they took advantage of the limelight, how they savoured and amplified each fresh narrative demanded by every new arrival at the corner shop!

Aunt Doll, who went to funerals as other people go to the pictures, knew she looked her best in black, and consequently attended the funerals of people she hardly knew, resplendent in second-hand black bombasine that she had acquired at a jumble sale. She would be unaware of the odd glances of puzzled relatives trying to place her in the ranks of their kin, and she enjoyed herself so much that she would forget where she was and put a cigarette in her mouth, absently striking a match on the side of a bier on which the coffin of a defunct grandfather swayed precariously and almost fell to the ground. She had a reputation for being sensitive and soft-hearted – based largely upon her ability to weep unrestrainedly at the sufferings of people like Little Willie and Maria Marten and upon her having been carried in a state of prostration from every place of entertainment in Northampton where such things were shown – but in real life she was always mistress of her grief at the misfortunes of others, grief that took second place to the rôle that she always assumed at such times of chief protagonist in the drama, prima donna, star turn. How could we be aware of other people's lives when we had always to be the principal personage in them? The people of Green Street needed help that no one was able to give. And even if anyone had been capable of offering such help, it is unlikely that they would have known how to receive it. It would have been like the embarrassing gifts of numberless loose-meshed kettleholders and dishcloths knitted by the old and inactive, which lay strewn uselessly about every kitchen in the street.

4. An Evening in 'The Garibaldi'

Every Saturday night for half a century the women of Green Street gathered in the Snug of 'The Garibaldi'. It was a time of intimacy and relaxation, a time for mutual commiseration and sympathy, a time for gossip and scandal. But it became something else too. It became a time for self-justification against the outside world: among the peeling brown paint and the frosted glass and the stained wooden tables, their conversation evolved into a declaration of faith in themselves and the standards they lived by, an exposition of their profoundest beliefs and thoughts.

They greet each other with inquiries about their health and their family. The woman who had an operation ten years ago returns to it unfailingly. 'I'm bin ever so middling agen this week, but then what can y'expect after a packet like that?', but nobody pays any attention to her as she continues, 'Had to come away you see it did, the whole bag o' tricks. 'Tain't the sort o' thing you can expect to get over in five minutes.' They know she mustn't be indulged or she'll talk about it all night, so the conversation is adroitly turned to someone else. 'How's your mother keepin', Mrs Carter?'

'Well, you know, it's her age more'n anythink else.'

'Ow old is she now?'

'Eighty-three in the noo year. She's a bit of a trial, though.'

'Well, you're bound to be at that age.'

'Poor ole soul.'

'Yis, one foot in the grave, gal, one foot in the grave ... 'Ad to laugh though yis'day – our Sandra said: yis she might be got one foot in the grave, but she's got the other bugger pretty firm in Green Street.'

'Don't 'spect she can get about much.'

'Sometimes she guz as fur as the Old Folks' Rest Centre. I'm thankful to see the back of 'er sometimes. She says she's got a long enough rest comin' as it is. Says she wun't see another winter after this 'un. Still, she's bin sayin' that for the last ten year.'

Mrs Carter says piously that she thinks sometimes it'd be a mercy if the old lady was Took, and she admits that her husband says it'll be a happy release for him when she is. 'I mean, we shouldn't gain by it, it'd mean losin' 'er pension.'

They drink up mournfully, and hope they won't linger to be a burden to anybody.

A melancholy reflective silence is established that can only be broken by a complete change of subject. Somebody mentions last week's television play, and they become suddenly animated.

'It was that bad we had to turn it off.'

'What was it?'

'Merchant o' Bloody Venice. Bloody Shakespeare.'

'O, 'im,' says another knowingly, as if she were talking about the carryings-on of some disreputable acquaintance.

'Somebody ought to write up,' interjects one woman vehemently – a frequent suggestion when they imagined themselves in any way wronged or slighted. It never went beyond the stage of suggestion, chiefly because they had not the faintest idea of whom to apply to for redress of their grievance.

'Sid says it's scandalous. All them men dressed up in tights and dinxin' about like a lot o' nancy-boys and spoutin' a lot o' poetry.' There is a muttered echo of agreement, 'bloody poetry'. She gains confidence in her theme, and pursues it indignantly. 'He reckons this age 'll goo down in 'Ist'ry as the Omerseckshul Age. An' 'e ain't far wrong, if you ask me.' (This belief was understandable in view of the changes in attitude towards homosexuality within her own lifetime. She had seen it shift from something associated with wide-eyed horror and incredulity, shame and gas-ovens to a subject for detached amusement. As the severity with which it was regarded diminished, it became more apparent, and although she could not know it, spotting queers and lezzies in the Saturday shopping crowds is one of the more innocent diversions of her own teenage sons.)

'Did you see it, Mrs Watts? Just up your street, I bet, all them men in tights.'

'Goo on, she's too old for that, ain't yer, gal?'

'Don't you be so sure.'

'Still waters run deep, eh, Ida?'

They talk of poetry and art as if it were a conspiracy against them. Somebody remembers having read of a painting by 'that ole b. Picasso' which was sold for many thousands of pounds. 'I said to our Jack, "How would you like that b. starin' at you all day?" ' he said, "There's only one room in the house it's fit for," I said, "Well if that didn't make you goo nothing ever would." '

Mrs Plackett says that her husband wouldn't let her switch off *The Merchant of Venice*, and they turn towards her in sympathy. 'He says it's ever so good when you get to know the ins and outs of it.' They stare at her, startled and incredulous, waiting for elucidation of this novel and unexpected response. But she is unable to account for it, and finishes apologetically, 'But then 'e's always bin a bit funny that way.'

'They don't know what it is to enjoy theirselves, people like that, do they?'

'I tell yer straight, gal' – and the drink releases long-re-pressed bitterness and tears of self-pity – 'and I don't care 'oo 'ears me say it' (an expression they always used prefatory to defiance of any accepted ideas) 'I wouldn't wish me worst enemy 'usband like I'm 'ad. I don't know 'ow I'm managed to stick it all these years. Our Geraldine says she'd 'ave divorced 'im long ago. Mental cruelty she says they call it. She makes no bones about it. 'E ain't bin no 'usband to me. . . .'

There is consternation among those assembled, less from a feeling of sympathy with what she must have suffered at the hands of a husband with highbrow pretensions, than from an awareness that she has introduced a topic that is not included in the area of public discussion. Someone tells her sharply to pull herself together, and she subsides on the bench against the wall, embarrassed by the sudden realization that she has exceeded the bounds of propriety. The conversation becomes broken and disjointed. They had no response to unforeseen personal disclosures. Ritual public mourning and rejoicing marked the limit of their involvement with others. A stony incomprehension greeted everything else. If you suffered, you were expected to show resignation and fortitude, and to present the outsiders the uniform imperturbability of the rest of the street, who were released from any obligation to sympathize with you by the prudent and comforting belief that all suffering was self-inflicted anyway, and therefore a result of your own folly or wickedness. You had only yourself to blame. If a husband were cruel you shouldn't have married him, if your children were unloving you had failed to bring them up properly, if you were ill you were guilty of neglect, and a determined stoicism was the only admissible attitude.

'Other people's troubles', like other people's kids and other people's houses, were their own concern. A woman – a stranger – once collapsed on the pavement in the middle of Green Street. The indignant householder, whose doorstep had been selected for this act of negligence, trembled and fluttered behind her lace curtain for some minutes before offering the afflicted stranger asylum within her house. Afterwards, when the ambulance had transported the sick woman to hospital, and she saw her property undefiled by the fleeting presence of a stranger who had had a heart attack, she confided to the neighbours that she had been terrified. 'I was frit to death she was gunner die on me,' as though it had been a premeditated action, and she carefully singled out as its victim.

People had to be discouraged from attempts to share their problems with you, or you might be forced to learn of whole unsuspected spheres of human suffering that would undermine everything you knew about human behaviour and experience.

They restore the disorbited conversation to its intended trajectory, with the panic and desperation with which they chase the escaped pet budgerigar as it flutters uncontrollably around the room and threatens to disappear through an open window. They turn to some sex crimes reported in the newspapers, and at once harmony and unanimity are restored among them. Mrs Plackett is the most shrill-tongued of all. She hopes that her extreme conformity and orthodoxy on this subject will obliterate the memory of her earlier misbehaviour.

'Yer kids ain't safe, are they, wi' people like that allowed to go roamin' the streets.' They believed that their children were the chosen prey of the millions of sexual deviationists they imagined peopled the outside world. Leaning forward confidentially, Poll Davies whispers hoarsely, 'If it's them sort o' things you want you don't need to goo lookin' in the noospapers.'

Their heads close over the table like the petals of a flower at the approach of rain. 'Oodjer mean? . . . Not . . . ?'

'Yis. Marlene Smith.' She looks round in order to ascertain that nobody is listening. 'Mrs Murwell told me she was gooin' past the bus shelter last night, and she just 'appened to glance in . . . And there were Marlene Smith . . .' She pauses dramatically, and looks from one to the other. '. . . with 'er skirt right up over 'er 'ead.' The petals separate as the sun comes out, and they nod to each other. Then one of them challenges her.

' 'Ow did she know it was Marlene Smith if her skirt was right over her head?'

Poll is annoyed by this irrelevancy. 'Well, it couldn't 'ave bin *right* over.'

'Well, you 'ave surprised me. Ever such a soft-spoken little girl she always seemed. Ever so quiet.'

Poll assumes an air of great wisdom and worldliness. 'It's allus the bloody quiet ones as are the worst.'

'Oo was she with, then?'

' 'E was a lorry driver.'

'I 'spect she could tell that an' all by just lookin' in the bus shelter.'

Poll says firmly, ' 'Is lorry were parked not twenty yards away. She's man-mad, that girl. Man-mad.'

One of the women is puzzled. 'She can't be all there . . . I mean . . . to stop a lorry just like that . . . She wouldn't even know wot 'e was like.'

Poll throws back her head and closes one eye. She speaks

again with insight and authority, as one to whom no extreme
of human conduct is in any way mysterious or inexplicable.
'That sort don't . . . Still she comes from a very funny fam'ly.
'Er mother's brother, look at 'im for a start. 'E 'ad a kink. I
shall say so long as I live.'

'Oh? Wot sort of a kink?'

'I don't know. 'E wadn't right. 'E used to sit down be the
Mill as they used for a bathin' place till little Wendy Merton
were drowned there, an' 'e useder be there from one end o'
the summer to the other . . . Just near where the kids useder
get undressed.'

Exclamations of shock and disbelief and pleasure. A frisson
of anticipation as they lean forward to catch her words.

'I useder say to our Roge, "Don't you goo near the Mill if
Sid Boorman's 'angin' about." ' Then she cries, suddenly vin-
dictive, ' 'E oughder bin put away.'

'You can't start puttin' people away just for sittin' down be
the bathin' place, Poll, my gel.'

'Peuh. There's never smoke without fire.'

'Still, you've only gotter look at that Marlene's mother.
She's only ninepence in the shillin'.'

'Well, there you are, then,' says Poll, by way of explanation.
' 'Er ole woman was the same, she acted as if she'd bin put in
wi' the bread an' pulled out wi' the cakes. She was that damn
mean she wouldn't give the drippin's of 'er nose away on a
frosty mornin'.'

'There but for the grace o' God, Poll my gel . . .', admonishes
a neighbour, but by now she has turned her attentions upon
Dopey Freda. Since the death of her parents she has been
working in the clothing factory at the top of the street. She has
been visited once or twice a week by a man in a car, and has
been paying him money towards the house which he assures
her he is having built for them to live in after their marriage.

'Silly b.,' says Poll, 'lettin' him put it across her like that.
Djou know what she told me this week? She said she's gunner
call her first child Clive if it's a boy, and Sharon if it's a girl. I
said to 'er I know what I call it if you have babies at your age, I
call it a miracle.'

Someone protests that Freda cannot help not having all her buttons.

'Peuh,' snorts Poll contemptuously, 'she shouldn't be so damn soft. She wun't get no sympathy out o' me.' She spoke as if the world were full of a more dangerous and implacable kind of enemy who sought to make your sympathy flow like blood. They knew and wanted to know nothing more of human behaviour than its surface manifestations, and upon these they based all their judgements. It sufficed for Poll to establish that someone was a thief, a liar, a whore, and, once this had been done, nothing more remained to be said. Stealing, mendacity or whoredom were the result of a perverse and wilful espousal of evil for its own sake. She could not imagine circumstances in which any of these things could be understandable, let alone forgivable. Poll's strictures upon Freda's gullibility, Marlene Smith's immorality, show that she is not interested in causes or explanations ('excuses' she would call them). She believes that the character of a human being is to be derived from his actions, and not the contrary. It is as though with every new action people created their character afresh, out of nothing; as though each individual were devoid of any prior experience when he came to act, and every step he took were isolated, independent of the one that preceded it; as though all human movement were not the result of an inextricable tangle of anguish and conflict, of hope and despair.

Because nearly everyone in the street resembled everybody else, at least in the outward appearance of his life, that sameness represented virtue, rightness, decency, and those who departed from it only did so out of 'wickedness' – a designation which shrouded real motives as effectively as earth shrouds the dead. This had to be believed so that everything might be classified in the sharply differentiated categories of absolute good and evil. There could be no admixture, no alloy. And to ensure that there should be none, they adapted, selected, truncated, mutilated every experience with no less scrupulousness than the most dedicated artist. By disregarding all causes of human behaviour, it was possible to make everything accord with their view of human life. But it did not help them to understand each other. It did not help them to rise to each other's needs, to allay one another's suffering, to assuage the secret and silent pain which almost every house in the street concealed.

Poll's fury against Marlene Smith and the man at the bathing-place derives perhaps less from a real sense of moral outrage than from an inchoate suspicion of the inadequacy of her own facile assessment of others. They present her with the idea that there may be something she does not know, and that other people may be subject to impulses and urges different from those which prompt her to act as she does. She feels therefore that if she is able to affix a name to anything that shocks or disturbs her, if she can say, 'That is a lie', 'That is a piece of deceit', 'That is murder', she has magically explained away all there is to know, just as when she was younger it was a popular pastime to catch dragonflies or moths and still the agitated beating of their wings by driving pins through their heads. . . .

Now Ede Rowell is talking about the blacks who have moved in next door. She invokes the spirit of the previous occupant, who had polished her letterbox and blackleaded her grate and dusted the piano every day without fail 'even though it was never touched since her mother passed on'. (Symbolic actions of this kind were very common. When Emily Wood's fiancé was killed in the First War she locked away her wedding presents in an upstairs room, where they were discovered after her death forty years later by astonished workmen, wide-eyed at the sight of this accumulation of household utensils no longer in use – tarnished fire-bellows and rusty pot-hooks, bottles of evaporated fluids for cleaning brass and lead, embroidered fire-screens and iron bedsteads.)

'If she could see it now she'd 'ave a fit, 'cos she was allus ever so partic'lar.' The worst of her successors' crimes is having replaced the flaking brown paint by a free application of scarlet and daffodil yellow. 'You wannear 'em singin' at night, all the bangin' an' the oola-loola. We reckon there's about twenny on 'em live next door to us, but you can't tell 'cos they all look the same. I said to Reg yis'day, "Oo look," I said, "it's snowin'," 'e said, "snowin'?", I said "Come an' 'ave a look at this" ... Djou know wot they was doin'? They were pluckin' chickens out o' the bedroom winder, it was all over the show, just like a bloody snowstorm. ... We don't say nothin' to 'em. ... They looks as if they could get very nasty. ...'

Another woman interrupts tentatively. 'Although Mrs Robinson always says they was ever so good to 'er up at th' 'ospital when she 'ad 'er operation.' They recognize this contribution as the single dissenting voice, put forward only to serve as foil to a vehement reaffirmation of their own real opinion. She knew no one would suspect her of liberal views. She fulfilled a necessary rôle in their assemblies, that of devil's advocate, for their opinions were so uniform and predictable that all dialogue would have ceased within five minutes if nobody had been present to supply contrary and contestable ideas.

'Mrs Robinson says the nurses was ever so gentle an' that.'

'Well our Sid was in there six weeks 'avin' 'is bit o' trouble seen to, an' 'e said 'e didn't mind 'em in the day time when you could see where they was, but at night you could only see the eyes, frit 'im to death. 'Cos o' course they don't make no noise when they move, no, it's a fact they don't,' she adds parenthetically as a movement of doubt spreads among her listeners, 'an' he never knoo where they was gunn appear next.'

'Well, when Ted Scrivens went over to Wolver'ampton for the match last week, 'e said 'im an' 'is missis wenn in a caff, and this woman – blackie, need you ask – come and sit down at the next table, and bold as brass she undone 'er dress and started givin' the kid the breast.'

'Well, there ain't nothin' to make a song an' dance about in that ... 'S bin gooin' on ever since I can remember.'

'You wait while I tell you ... 'Fore she started, djou know what she done?' She challenges them one by one. 'Well, she dipped 'er breast in the sugar basin ... Yis, it's true as I sit 'ere ... I said to 'im, "Didn't yer do nothin'?", 'e said, "Yis, we walked out," I said, "Walked out," I said, "I'd a-kicked up such a stink she'd a-thought twice about doin' it agen. ..."'

'Well,' says someone, conciliatory, 'you can't expect 'em to be like us ... It's took us years, ain't it, centuries like, to get where we are ...'

The arrival of coloured people in the street coincided with the first signs of internal disintegration of life there in its traditional changeless uniformity. The street had never known human beings who lived by standards other than its own. The only outsiders they knew of were the rich, and the hatred which they bore them derived as much from their foreign and outlandish values as from the mere fact of their wealth : it was their 'poshness', their social manner, the idleness of their womenfolk that were really hated − social differences. Any social differences would have provoked the same enmity, because of the inadmissibility of any other way of life than that which existed in the street. The first Negroes appeared to them as an embodiment of the dawning idea that the life they had believed to be the only real human life was simply one possible life of many. They found suddenly that they were adherents of a dying faith, and became more clamorous and desperate in upholding its worth and meaning. Like a foetus in a protective caul, they were shielded by their faith against reality : the reality is that the existence of a plurality of beliefs robs them all of absolute significance. Faith grows with a man like a cortex or integument, but once it is pierced he is as helpless and tormented as a wounded man who watches a pool of blood drain away from his exsanguine form.

They begin to justify themselves against the disruptive forces they feel to be working against them.

'Nobody wun't do nothin' for us, gal. We only put this country where it is. We're the ones as won the war, ain't we, not all these bloody politicians.'

'They're all out for number one, gal.'

'They all piss in the same pot.'

'We're the ones as count. Not all these Dooks an' Royalty.'

'Salt o' the earth, the workin' man,' Poll pontificates. 'We're done what we was put 'ere for. Slavin' in a factory all week tryin' to bring up a fam'ly decent and proper... There ain't nobody can do more in life...' And she adds with finality, 'Nobody.'

'If there is I'd like to meet 'em.' But they all took good care not to.

'Not even the Queen of England. She's only the same as us. When all's said an' done she can only sleep in one bed, eat one dinner at a time and sit on one lav, can't she?'

'Aah.' Ellen Youl has been watching the movement of their lips, unable to hear anything because of her deafness, but following the conversation from memory. She may have missed some of the detail, but the basic order and structure of their exchanges have remained unchanged, like a scenario of the *commedia dell' arte* nailed to a pillar in the wings for the guidance of the actors. As the oldest one present, Ellen knows it is her turn to give them the benefit of her eighty-six years' experience of life in Green Street. 'I can truthfully say I'm never bin be'olden to nobody all me life long ... I'm never expected nothin' of other people and I'm never wanted 'em to expect nothin' o' me ... I'm kep' meself to meself and I'm never owed nobody 'alfpenny ... I'm never done nobody a bad turn and there ain't nobody on this earth I can't look straight in the eye ... An' if a foo more people could say as much, the world 'd be a damn sight 'appier place. ...'

They murmur their agreement, and all the negatives in her bleak view of the world go unnoticed.

They are interrupted by someone collecting for a wreath for May Rayson. 'Sat 'ere she did, week in, week out, for the best part o' forty year.' Nobody could sing "The Rose of Tralee' quite like she could, and nobody will again, at least not in 'The Garibaldi'. A melancholy silence is established, heightened by the sound of laughter from the bar and the clash of glasses. In an adjoining room the skittles fall and are set up again.

'Makes you wonder 'oo's gunner be next, dunnit?' The clamour is stilled for a moment as they look at each other. The falling flesh and thinning hair, swollen ankles and knotted hands. A woman pushes some strings of henna'd hair across her forehead, and another slouches forward on the hard stool. In the corner Granny Bray is crying silently into the dregs of her beer, and no one pays any attention to her because they think she is drunk. But she is crying because she remembers a Sunday afternoon in July that seemed to last for ever, cool beer in an enamel jug, the rickety wooden chair on the hot pavement, a ham tea and the voices of children. She cries not because she regrets it, but for no other reason than that she remembers; it may be the smell of the beer that releases it, and it rises up in her like a strong choking vapour, forcing the present into oblivion.

' 'Ardly seems possible, does it? I was talkin' to 'er only last Monday.'

'You're 'ere today and gone tomorrer.'

'And we ain't none of us gettin' no younger ... Look at me ... Lovely 'ead of 'air I used to 'ave – and she fingers her thin and tinted hair, gently, as though afraid of damaging it further by her touch – 'I could sit on it when I was twenty. But not now, gal, not now.'

'What about me? I used to be real bonny ... But you wouldn't think so today....' And she raises a thin bare arm. 'Where's it all gone?' They talk with fear and wonder, as though they had been disfigured by some stealthy and un-declared enemy, like virgins ravished as they slept.

'Oo, for God's sake snap out of it. Don't start gettin' morbid of a Sat'day night' – as though there were an appointed weekly cycle of grief and joy. And she goes to the piano, urging them to sing. They do as she bids them, and then engender a spuri-ous and artificial warmth. As they rock gently to and fro to the sound of the 'Merry Widow' Waltz, there is something hysteri-cal in their gaiety, in the contrived protraction of a way of living which they know to be superseded and in decline. . .

5. Kin

The ideas governing the relationships in street and neighbourhood formed a natural complement to the conception of family and blood-ties. Affection was meted out according to the precise degree of kinship, with the austerity of a miserly and pennywise grocer scooping out flour or rice from a sack with a measuring jug. It was never allowed to rise up in spontaneous response to the characteristics, the disposition or nature of the person involved.

The world is separated naturally into two insurmountable divisions – 'our own' and 'other people'. Our own (kinsfolk) fall into three groups. First of all there are those we love and cherish, often with grim and studied application, because of the proximity of the relationship. Then there is a wide circle of less close relatives, for whom we feel a moderate and controlled warmth, whom we visit regularly if not frequently, whom we do not hesitate to help if they are in trouble (provided that they can prove to our satisfaction that it is not self-inflicted), and whose funerals we attend, even if this involves an infringement of our carefully contrived timetable of visits. Finally, there are those on the periphery of the family consciousness, details of whose lives we are familiar with, but whose separation from us in time or space prevents personal intimacy.

But as for other people – we want no truck with them. If they suffer it's no concern of ours, if they are happy we want no part of their alien joy. And yet we cannot ignore them totally. Reluctantly exogamous, we are compelled from their number to choose a husband or wife who, after a protracted period of hostility and criticism, will finally be absorbed, like a food that is digested with difficulty, into the main body of our kin.

All girls taken home would be regarded with apprehension, and as soon as they opened their mouths their intruder's idiom and interloper's ways would be felt as an implied criticism of the family with its established rituals, its private lore and its common and incommunicable experience. A series of tactful and guarded questions, asked between genteel coughs and nervous tentative smiles over the best fluted bone china cups about their husbandry or thrift or housewifely ability, having met with off-hand or irreverent replies, the verdict would be pronounced against them. And yet if such girls, in spite of the cool welcome and long disapproving silences, persisted in their visits to the house, as the best china gave way to the plain everyday market cups, and as they moved from awkward teas uneasily installed on the slippery edge of the brass-studded leather three-piece in the parlour into the warmth and untidiness of the living-room, so the initial verdict of wifely inadequacy would transform itself into a grudging concession that with intense and sustained tutelage from a mother they might possibly acquire a sense of responsibility and a certain amount of domestic skill, and this in turn would yield to an infinite admiration for their ability and virtue, until they were at length assimilated, and ultimately indistinguishable from those born into our kin.

Only once did it happen that after the due cycle had been completed, a son-in-law unexpectedly showed his true colours and ran away with another woman. The family found its original distrust vindicated and they were all able to say with justification, 'I never liked him right from the start.' This was true, of course. They never liked *anybody* from the start. Those who claimed our friendship or affection – if indeed such people existed – clamoured in vain, like beggars and petitioners on the doorstep of a medieval despot. The family was completely self-reliant, and scorned social intercourse as a sign of weakness or inadequacy, something as shameful as an avowal of sexual dissatisfaction in marriage. We were not to be beguiled or distracted from the company of those who mattered,

our own, and anyone who sought to make contact with outsiders was accused of 'playing to the gallery'. The family was
like a plain and virtuous woman, at pains to display her
pudicity by perpetual denunciation of the meretricious lures
and enticements of a showy and shallow world which did not
interest her anyway.

For it was occasionally admitted that there could be something superficially attractive in other people. They could ap-
peal to weak or disloyal members of the family as a novelty or
entertainment, because it had to be acknowledged that all the
family's reactions, its views and experience were thoroughly
known to all, and would be reverted to at every assembly and
gathering with such predictability that they were entirely without excitement or spontaneity. Every memory, every story
would be recited like a play that has been performed too long
on the same stage. Sometimes, at ritual Christmas or other
festal meetings, the predictability of some story or event from
the past was felt to be its greatest charm, and faulty recital of a
familiar tale would bring protests from those who knew it well.
Any deviation from a fixed text caused the hearers to feel
cheated. Ellen Youl, talking of Cousin Ada's death: 'Right as
rain on the Friday night ... dead on the Monday mornin' ...
She came out o' work, said she never felt none too grand, went
into Woolworth's for a bit o' cake for the kids' tea ... Come
over queer ... Somebody took 'er 'ome, she was worse on the
Sat'day ... They rushed 'er to 'ospital on the Sunday night ...
Dead by the time they got 'er there. . . .'

This was delivered in exactly the same way each time, all
conjunctions suppressed, in a staccato voice, with long dramatic pauses between each detail. None of the stages of the
alarming and accelerated progression of her illness could be
eliminated. If any omission occurred, someone would be sure
to supply it at the end (for nobody ever interrupted). 'And she
went into Woolworth's for a bit of cake for the kids' tea, didn't
she?' they would ask anxiously, as if even things they knew to
have happened incontestably had been impaired or eroded
since their last narration. Occasionally, everybody present
would articulate the words of the story under their breath as

Ellen talked, perhaps voicing the last sentence in chorus with
her. When the tale had been concluded a gloomy and reflective
silence would fall, and this would invariably be followed by
some observations upon the insecurity and unpredictability of
human fortunes. Then someone would say that such uncer-
tainty was perhaps all for the best, because if we knew what
was going to happen we would spend all our time worrying
about it.

Any one of their set pieces, once uttered, determined the
course of the conversation for some time afterwards. It provoked the same responses every time, the same chains of
thought. The surprising thing was that nobody seemed to
notice that every phrase had been uttered before in an identical
context, and nobody protested at the constant reiteration of
dialogues and speeches they heard every time they met. None
of them ever evinced the slightest boredom. Perhaps from the
endless repetitions they derived some comfort, perhaps they
persuaded themselves that permanence and stability did exist
in a life that robbed them of their children in infancy, their
wives in childbed and their husbands at the height of their
strength and vigour. The interminable reiteration gave them an
illusion of security where there was none, and their conversations were repeated like recurring refrains in the games of
some impossibly old and worldly children.

Of the three groups of our kin, the first overshadows all the
rest. Our lives are inextricably bound up with theirs. For them
we sustain an unconditional and unvarying affection, quite independently of the kind of people they may be. Evidence of
this affection has to be shown in frequent visits to their home
and prolonged periods spent in their company.

Whenever two or three days passed without a visit from one
of my aunts, my mother would become restless and preoccupied until the overdue meeting had been accomplished. If
the rattle of the door-handle and the prelusive 'Yoo-oo' in the
passage announcing a visit were not heard, she would go to
them (none of them lived more than a few streets away), a
reproachful 'I thought I'd better come and have a look at you',

on her lips. This remark characterized quite literally many of their visits: they would sit and look at each other for an hour, and then go away again. Although they felt compelled to be together often, they knew they had nothing to say. They were frequently reduced to games of Newmarket or rummy for halfpennies to pass the time they were together, but it never occurred to any of them that they might have been more profitably or more enjoyably occupied in anyone else's company.

Because of the prescriptive nature of all our relationships, they were static and unchanging. We were fixed in attitudes towards other people as immovably as sculptured figures are fixed in stone. Sons and daughters never acquired adult status, but were stunted in perpetual childhood; brothers and sisters kept up a lifetime of dutiful and loveless fellowship.

Alice and Joe were regarded as models of marital concord and family orthodoxy. They spent sixty-five years together, and the chief bond between them was their shared hatred of everybody also. In fact this hatred was so intense and all-embracing that it always seemed incredible that two beings of their perfection ever contrived to meet in so base and iniquitous a world; and even more remarkable was the hazard that had placed them both at the same time in the closing room of Lewis's boot factory.

They had enemies everywhere. The street was full of 'nasty pieces of work', 'treacherous families', 'snakes in the grass', people who 'wouldn't do you a good turn if they could do you a bad one'. One neighbour in particular was always referred to as 'a very treacherous woman', and it was difficult not to wonder what possible source of danger they anticipated in the wizened little creature with her leather shopping-bag and darned woollen mittens and speedwell-blue eyes. (This was as baffling as the attitude of our own street towards two former prostitutes who frequented the neighbourhood, familiarly called Sickness and Diarrhoea, and who were said to have led lives of inexpressible wickedness. I remember looking at them and wondering how it was possible for anyone so old to have been wicked: their hair was grizzled and they walked arm in arm wherever they went, which seemed to betoken affection and helplessness rather than anything else. I was puzzled by the intangibility of their criminality; but in common with all the other children, imbued with fear of the two women's mysterious infectiousness, I held my breath and closed my mouth tightly whenever they walked by.)

Alice and Joe felt themselves victims of unceasing cabal and intrigue, and they imputed to the neighbours baleful powers that no human being could ever possess. People stopped talking whenever they passed by; children called after them in the street; shopkeepers gave them short measure and shoddy goods. Once Alice had found a rusty nail in a Bakewell tart, and as her teeth grated upon the metal over the frugal tea-table she remembered a scornful look in the shopgirl's eyes as she had handed her purchase over the counter. Alice's persuasion of the whole world's hostility had been reinforced by two major events in her life.

Once, a woman whose husband was in gaol ('where he belonged') had tried to borrow money. 'I don't know what she took me for,' said Alice with the grim chuckle that accompanied each recital of the incident, 'but she must a-bin at the end of her tether to think she'd get a penny-piece out o' me.' And then, in the same year, the next-door neighbour had thrown some bedsprings over the garden wall, which had flattened the pale waxen shoots of the kidney beans. (In the tiny back garden Alice and Joe kept up a kind of subsistence farming. They relied upon other people as little as it is possible to do so, living in the centre of a big town. They grew cabbages and brussels sprouts and beans and carrots which they ate with laboured and determined enjoyment, as though the appellation 'home grown' could magically transform the withered and blackened vegetables which they actually grew into rich and fleshy tubers.) Alice went immediately to the police, but it was not until many months later that she realized why her plaint had been disregarded. She overheard the neighbour say that she had a son-in-law in the police force. At this piece of intelligence they became terrified. The woman could use them as

she pleased and there would be no hope of redress. They cow-
ered fearfully indoors, waiting for further outrages. These
were not slow in coming. The radio was turned up to its max-
imum volume late at night, the blight on the lilac bush next
door was allowed to spread to the already damaged vegetable
patch, and Alice was frightened one night on her way to the
outdoor lavatory by a rat as long as her forearm, with the
result that she did not have the courage to use it again for a
month.

They rose and went to bed with the sun. 'No sense in burning daylight.' Their front door was kept permanently bolted,
and, apart from the family, their only visitors were gipsies and
the nuns collecting charity envelopes, for which they kept a
special hoard of foreign coins and large flat buttons. Alice was
too involved with her own illnesses to believe in the existence
of famine or leprosy. 'They wanner look after their own first.'
They never went out, and believed that anyone out of doors
after nine at night must be 'breaking the law or whore-hop-
pin''.

Alice was always ill. She spoke of digestive tracts and ali-
mentary canals as other people speak of geographical features
of countries they have visited. Whenever members of the family called to see her they were expected to ask solicitously,
'How's your belly?', as if it were a cherished and symbiotic
thing with a separate existence. The doctors never knew, or
wouldn't tell her, what was the matter with her, and the
miracle of her survival from day to day was the inexhaustible
theme of all her conversation.

If the couple's distrust and peevishness against the outside
world had been balanced by a genuine attachment and sympathy between them, this might have redeemed the rigour and
austerity of their lives. It is true that they shared the same bed
for sixty-five years; that they fulfilled the family's requirements of duty towards each other; but their long time together
was a time of silence, as they sat one on either side of the
barely smouldering coals in the hearth, she making rugs from
pieces of old coats and skirts in the chlorotic green light from
the single gas-mantle, he devising imaginary games of draughts

with absent opponents, eating dry seedcake, with barley water to flush out their kidneys.

Occasionally I was left at their house while my mother went shopping. Every time they served the same meal, baked potatoes, floating in a dark gravy covered with oily globules and surrounded by a piecrust as black and hard as the tin it was cooked in. Every time I refused to eat it, and they would try to force me into submission with the same piece of dialogue:

'He'll never grow up big and strong, will he, Joe?'

'Not if he don't eat his pudden.'

'He's lucky to be got it, ain't he, Joe?'

'We wouldn't a-wanted a lot o' beggin' and prayin' when we was his age.'

'Well, we wadn't given the chance, was we?'

'Prairie pudden was all we got, wadn't it?'

'Djou know what prairie pudden is?'

'It means the wide open spaces.'

'In other words, bugger all.'

All of their conversations were like this. One of them would start a sentence, the end of which would be supplied by the other, and they appealed to each other for support in their most trivial observations, 'Didn't I, Mother?', 'Wasn't I, Joe?' They were constantly deflected from whatever they were discussing into endless wrangles about whether it had been on Tuesday or Wednesday that Mrs Tapp had given them that nasty look in Bouverie Street, or whether it had been three o'clock or nearer half past when they went into the butcher's and were sold that piece of bad meat. They no longer recalled to which of them certain things had happened, and the same event – a stay in hospital or a fall on the ice – was sometimes claimed by both of them as part of their own experience. Their personalities had fused together, merged like rivers flowing over an even terrain with no obstacle to divide them.

Not all family ritual was as arid and dismal as the lives of Alice and Joe, confined within a relationship as cramped and claustral as their dark basement kitchen. When it was known that my mother's sister had leukaemia and could not live through the summer, all her immediate kin instinctively sus-

pended their own lives, and turned automatically towards her.
For a brief spell she was allowed to become the centre of their
existence. All her wishes were indulged, all her needs attended
to. From the frequency of their visits she was able to assess the
seriousness of her illness, and to calculate the length of time
remaining to her. She recognized the rite in which she herself
had taken part many times, making it easy for the dying person, bearing him gently towards death by creating an atmosphere, an illusion of life and gaiety all around him. The intention was to render incredible to the patient the idea that life
could possibly cease for him. The tenderness and care with
which she was treated only confirmed May in the certainty of
what was happening to her. She was fed with all kinds of
gossip and news and distractions. Problems were invented so
that her advice might be sought, she was conferred with and
consulted about decisions which she could never live to benefit
from. Her kinsfolk, as if aware of their past shortcomings and
the failure to maintain at the required intensity the affection
due to close relatives, tried to force a lifetime's regard and
solicitude into a few months. When the funeral was over one
of her sisters said that if any of the family really believed the
tales with which they comforted each other about meeting
again in an afterlife, and if they were really convinced by the
obituary rhymes which they caused to appear in the local
newspaper about sleeping where no shadows fall, and being
called home and leaving earth's foreign strand, they would not
have needed to go to such lengths to console the dying upon
their approaching departure from this life. And she concluded
that the delights of heaven were a good deal less certain than
the rattle of the dry July earth on a wooden coffin.

One woman, unhappily married and with two children,
made the mistake of confessing to her sister an attachment
that she had formed with a man she had known before her
marriage, and who visited her three times a week while her
husband was away. The sister decided that it was her duty to
arrange all her visits to coincide with the arrival of the lover,
in order to prevent the liaison from developing into anything

more dangerous or compromising. Whenever the man was at the house, the sister would appear also, accompanied by the children whom she had found in the park or the street, where they had been sent to play. She ensured that the erring couple were never left alone, until at length the fancy-man, intimidated by the ubiquitous sister, finally made off, and the unhappy marriage remained otherwise undefiled. The woman was at first very angry but, as time went by, she was heard to declare frequently and with increasing vehemence that no happiness was to be found outside the wedding ring, which may have been because she had been convinced by her sister's insistence, or it may have been because – and this is more likely – having been thwarted in her own search for happiness outside it, she had become clamorous and passionate in her support of the moral order.

The breaking up of illicit or adulterous relationships was a task which any close blood relation was by tacit consent entitled to assume, since forbidden connections represented a threat to the order and stability of the family group. Many women derived a good deal of drama and self-importance from such avocations. They would arrive at the house of the guilty party with a great sense of occasion and dressed in their best, disclaiming any self-interest or pleasure in the undertaking (which, to anyone who saw them at such times, was a lie) and justifying their presumptuousness by saying that if they had not taken it upon themselves no one else would have done so. They would be offered refreshment by the wrongdoer, and would decline, indicating the serious nature of their mission by the refusal of the tainted offering, and showing that they were not to be waylaid or distracted from carrying out what they had to do. If the wrongdoers refused to acknowledge the impropriety of their conduct and persisted in the unlawful relationship, the family would feel justified in casting them off completely and implacably. After such expulsions, sisters have lived next door to each other for thirty years without speaking, and only giving sign of themselves by means of a kettle of boiling water thrown over a trespassing cat, or the percussion of pots and saucepans late at night.

It was in the total merging of our own lives with the lives of our near kin that an explanation may be found for the resentful and uncharitable attitude towards other people. By endowing outsiders with a malevolence which they were probably far from feeling, we absolved ourselves from any obligation of involvement with them. If we were to commit ourselves to them as unreservedly as we did to 'our own', there would be no limit to the demands upon our compassion and sense of duty, and so the pretence was assiduously maintained that they were not worth knowing. In this way any close contact that might have proved the contrary was avoided. If a member of the family disputed any of the lore about other people's selfishness and ill-will – for instance the belief that if you invited your neighbours to set foot inside your house you would have the greatest difficulty in ever getting rid of them again – he would provoke the greatest hostility and be made to feel disloyal and treacherous. The attention which we bestowed upon our nearest and dearest (which they often were not) was so all-absorbing and intense that it could never extend to more than half a dozen people at the most. If the families were very large – as Ellen Youl's was – they would divide themselves yet further for protection and warmth. Ellen's three youngest daughters formed an unassailable faction, while her four oldest children were quite inseparable. This left the central group – who had little in common – exposed, and consequently forced them to ally themselves into a third unwilling coterie.

Obligations were always discharged out of a sense of necessity in direct proportion to the closeness of the relationship, and we were always on our guard against being drawn towards people by sympathy and inclination. Often these haphazard assemblages of human beings, united only by common parentage and a highly developed sense of duty towards each other, lived out their lives in boredom and dissatisfaction, and sometimes in mutual hatred. Defections were very rare, notwithstanding the unceasing threat of mothers to selfish husbands and ungrateful children that they would arrive home one day and find them missing. 'If you do that once more' (referring to anything that incurred their anger, from a child's misbehaviour to a husband's adultery) 'I'll put my hat and coat on and walk through that door and never come back.' But they never did. And they used the threat so often that it soon ceased to have any effect upon those it was intended to chasten or frighten into compliance and co-operation. They knew she would always be there, querulous and oppressed, until the children were married and the husband's obduracy and churlishness were tempered by time and she forgot the pain they had caused her.

When D. discovered that her husband had been using his job as long-distance lorry driver to visit a woman in Coventry, she did not leave him. Nothing changed in her outward behaviour. She continued to set his meals before him, to clean his shoes and exchange necessary domestic conversation as before, but the rancour accumulated like a sediment within her, undisturbed by the formal discharge of what she considered an inescapable duty. There were many people like her, performing actions and deferring to principles which destroyed and deadened their sensibility, stifled their emotions and prevented any avowal of what they really thought and felt.

In Bouverie Street two sisters lived next door to each other. Kate, the younger, had made a successful marriage, and she could not resist flaunting her happiness before Daisy, her sister, who had had the misfortune to marry a man as cruel and violent as he was mean. Her sister's success vexed and repelled her, but the closeness of their relationship compelled them to see much of each other and to simulate sisterly concern and interest in each other's family. Kate had three children who were all as fortunate as their mother, all intelligent, of friendly address and complaisant disposition. The older boy became a schoolteacher, and the girl a hairdresser. Daisy, as if vying with her sister, had four children, none of whom brought her any joy. Two of them died in infancy, of diphtheria, and of the two who survived, one was a rickety and ill-favoured girl who mortified her mother yet further by remaining unmarried, and the other a boy who had inherited his father's perverse and disputatious character and was permanently in trouble with the police. As Kate prospered, so her sister's hatred gathered strength and her envy grew. Kate was complacent and self-congratulatory, and never ceased talking about the prodigious endowments and attainments of her offspring. Daisy was constrained by family convention to parody a delight in the accomplishments of her nephews and niece equal to that of her sister, whom she could never hear speak without imagining that every conversation was intended merely to underline her own misery.

At length their husbands died, and not long afterwards Kate had a stroke which disabled her completely. She recovered sufficiently to live a further three years, but she became very fat and her brain had been impaired by a clot of blood. (That she survived at all was pronounced by the doctors to be a miracle, and in consequence of this distant members of the family arrived at her house to view the woman who'd had a clot of blood pass through her brain and had lived, although they had not the slightest notion of the significance or medical details of the 'miracle' involved.) She was not able to fend for herself in any way. Her memory deteriorated; she lost the use of her limbs, and had to be wheeled about in an invalid chair. Naturally enough this task fell to Daisy, who had to all appearance evinced a sustained sisterly affection over the years. She decided that the time had come to be revenged. One day she took her sister into town, ostensibly to buy her some new clothes, which indeed she did. She decked her in garish pinks and yellows, made up her face with rouge and powder and lipstick, clipped diamanté rings to her pendulous ear-lobes and pearls around her sagging chin, and set a great brooch at her tumid and distended breast. Kate submitted to this transformation trustingly, unknowingly, smiling and nodding at the passers-by like a huge bedridden prostitute. Daisy had repressed her feelings for so long that when the hated woman fell at last into her power, she could not resist the opportunity of humiliating and ridiculing her, although her victim was not able to appreciate the outrage committed against her impotence and infirmity. The family was aghast at Daisy's vindictiveness, and they rejected her finally and remorselessly. In aggravation of this breach of family loyalty, it was discovered that she had been helping herself to Kate's pension money, which she had been drawing for twelve months, guiding her sister's bloated and useless hand to form an erratic signature.

A husband and wife had lived in dissension all their married life. When the husband died his widow declared her intention of donating the body to medical research, averring that this had been his last wish. Of course nobody believed her. It was partly an act of meanness to save the funeral expense, and partly a final triumph in the long conjugal dispute. The body was dispatched to the University of Birmingham, and she was heard to say publicly that she hoped they pulled the old sod to bits. She was outraged to receive a bill for the interment of his remains after his corpse had been duly dissected and analysed. She complained of an unfeeling intrusion into her grief and purse. She was felt by the family to have been justly dealt with, and they never forgave her this unheard-of piece of meanness any more than they forgot the infringement of family convention which her disrespect for her husband's corpse represented. The family's care of its kin extended a long way beyond death. The ceremonial laying-out and dressing of the body was often a source of contention among the survivors, as was the order of 'following' at the funeral, the preparation of the funeral victuals, the pilgrimages to the grave, the cutting of the grass around it and the supply of fresh flowers, and the annual insertion of the *In Memoriam* in the paper to proclaim to people who didn't know us that we did not forget our kin two or five or even ten years after parting from them.

6. Portrait of a Marriage

The women of our family were nothing but physiological phenomena. They bore children and effaced themselves, hoping perhaps that the pointlessness of their own lives might be offset by the achievements of the following generation, which, however, invariably proved to be as passive and indecisive as themselves. They strove to be worthy of the preceding generation by making life easier for the next one. Their present was poisoned by the fear of failing to live up to the past and of neglecting their duty to the future. They were immured in the role of wife and mother, and if a woman displayed interest in a career or abandoned an indifferent husband for a lover, she was thought to be irresponsibly selfish. They were inexhaustibly fascinated by their capacity for motherhood, and boasted unceasingly of the pain they had endured and the difficulty they had experienced giving birth. In order to gain the esteem of their children, and because childbirth was their only accomplishment, they impressed upon them that they 'had been in labour for the best part of twenty-four hours' or that 'the doctor said I'd never rear you'. If children failed to share their mother's evaluation of themselves (which rarely happened – mothers were always talked of with almost religious reverence, and were 'saints on earth' or 'goodness itself'), the aggrieved mother, who had grown old in the service of her children, held them responsible for the ageing process itself. 'You needn't say you don't want me,' Ellen Youl would say when she was out of temper with her sons and daughters, 'just because I'm got a few lines on me face, 'cause you put 'em there.' Growing old was a humiliation to which she had consented in order to earn their gratitude.

Until they married, women had no opinions or convictions

at all. For a girl to have expressed independent ideas would have been as disgraceful as to boast of pre-marital sex. In this way, her mind remained virgin for whatever ideas her man should decree, which she would then adopt to a degree of intensity decreed by her consort.

Tom arrived in Green Street from Daventry when he was twenty, and he found lodgings with old Sarah above her second-hand clothes shop. But people did not live in lodgings in Green Street, and single men over twenty-five, unless they belonged to an established street family, were unknown. He saw our Mary in the street one day, as she was wheeling out a sister's baby. He challenged her peremptorily. 'That kid your'n?' She said that it wasn't. 'That's all right, then,' and he walked on. Within three months they were married.

Tom came of the same peasant stock as our family. They kept a grocery store in Daventry. They were superstitious, sparing and penurious, profoundly conservative, and had a great respect for their betters. Tom's mother would sit in a rocking chair among the willow-herb and lavender and mint in the yard behind the house, and watch the sheet lightning ripen the corn. Once a rick took fire in a neighbouring field, and she nodded her head and warned that many such fires could be expected during the course of the summer. When asked how she knew, she smiled scornfully and said, 'Well, the sun shone all last Christmas Day, didn't it?' When Tom took his wife home for the first time, they surveyed her critically, were impressed, and bestowed upon her the highest praise they could give. 'She's all right. She's got a pair of shoulders on her as gentry'd be proud on.' (They were convinced of the physical perfection of the gentry and of their immunity from bodily deterioration. Whenever Royalty visited the area, they would look wonderingly upon an elderly queen or princess and see not a wrinkle, not a blemish. 'She hasn't aged a bit, has she?' they would say reverentially, still half believing in the immortality of the great, their divine origin.)

Tom's mother had been in service with Lady C., who graciously patronized the shop of her former housemaid. Whenever the bill was sent (which was frequently – Lady C. did not share the financial scrupulousness of her erstwhile domestic), it was always accompanied by a note apologizing for the necessity of sending it, and signed 'Yours very respectfully'. They always took money deprecatingly, and with calculated indifference, and gave to understand that they only did so under compulsion from a higher authority, and that if they had their own way all the goods in the shop would be free. This did not prevent them from keeping their money in the hollow knob of a brass bedstead, in a room permanently locked, the key of which Tom's mother wore on a black bootlace round her neck.

They had a deep sense of their own inferiority, but, far from giving rise to any resentment, it was the origin of great satisfaction and complacency. Whenever they came into contact with their superiors, their very presence in the same room or street was such an inconceivable felicity that it threw them into a state of panic. They would fidget and laugh hysterically, and apologize for the clothes they were wearing or the way they spoke. I was once with Tom's father in the town's main street when we met Lady C. Immediately the old man began to cover his soiled brown denim smock with his arms, like a woman surprised bathing. He displayed an infantile pleasure when she reassured him of the dignity of toil, and he talked of nothing else all the way home. They were persuaded that their imperfections must give offence to their exalted interlocutor. On the occasions when Lady C. actually entered the shop, Tom's mother would snatch off her apron, stammer and tremble, and insert many irrelevant and breathy aspirates and ma'ams into her speech. She always held her hand in front of her mouth as she spoke, as though she expected it to disgorge toads or a flow of black bile. Once the ordeal was over, it became a reason for self-importance for days afterwards. 'We'll have some nice dried peas for tomorrow's dinner. Lady C. likes dried peas.' Until that time she had frequently referred to dried peas as a dish beneath her consideration, being neither tasty nor nourishing.

Not only did they never doubt the validity of their ordered and harmonious view of society, but it occasionally had also great practical advantages. Tom's father spent any free time he could spare from the shop beating the bushes for a local retired colonel during the shooting season, and when he was once charged with a poaching offence, the magistrate proved to be the landowner for whom he had spent the whole of the preceding weekend hunting out pheasants and partridge from the undergrowth. The expected heavy fine did not materialize.

They were mean. Of them it was said that 'they'd bottle a fart and use it again if they could'. Tom's mother was extremely reluctant to throw away anything she had used personally, and even left the water she had washed in cooling greyly for hours in the enamel bowl in the sink. Once they found some mice-droppings in a sack of flour, and they spent the whole night extracting the tiny black grains from the bag before offering the tainted powder for sale the following morning. They 'couldn't abide waste', to the extent, some members of the family suggested, of raking through their own excreta to see if there was anything worth having. They talked of setting aside a little something for their old age until they were well into their eighties, and then old age was upon them and they died still providing for it. They had made no will, not believing that death could supervene before the rainy day which they had spent their whole life anticipating. They worked in the shop unremittingly, hopelessly, and stayed open even on Bank Holidays and Christmas Day. They worked like characters in a fairy tale, who every day had been set an impossible feat by a supernatural taskmaster who would return at sunset to claim some terrible forfeit if the allotted work had not been carried out. They employed a series of assistants whom they addressed by the hereditary title of 'Johnny-me-lad', and who rode a huge rusty bicycle bearing the name of his employers on a black metal panel set within the framework, and whose wastefulness (another inherited characteristic) they swore would be the ruin of them. (This rôle of assistant resembled the rôle of neighbours in the streets: like Johnny-me-lad, a neighbour was a fixed and predictable phenomenon which was never modified by the characteristics of the various individuals who assumed it.)

Tom and Mary were the first members of both families to develop a critical attitude to the ideas and values of the past. In neither family had there been any radical tradition. Others had successfully emancipated themselves by 'marrying well' like Aunt Laura in Leicester, or by 'making their way in the world', but until that time it seems not to have occurred to any of them that they might be able to influence ideas or living conditions as they found them. Ashamed of the inertia and passivity of their forbears, Tom (and by contagion his wife) frequented organizations for the material and spiritual advancement of the people. Some of their enthusiasm even affected other members of the family, but it did not last long with most of them, and the only remaining evidence of their fleeting zeal is a residual tendency to vote Labour if they can remember the name of the candidate and some dog-eared editions on cheap paper of *Intelligent Women's Guides*, *Merrie England* and the works of H. G. Wells, long consigned to cardboard boxes on top of the wardrobe with other sentimental relics and curios, school prizes and Mabel Lucie Attwell birthday cards and wedding photographs of brides invisible behind cloche hats and feather boas. In their brief period of political consciousness our family was no different from many others. For generations they had slumbered on in post-feudal torpor, like some powerful primitive beast, which towards the end of the last century stirred uneasily in its secular slumber, rose up and emitted a long angry howl, and then lay down and went to sleep again. Then it slept the brutalized sleep of ignorance and despair, but now it sleeps the sleep of satiety and contentment.

Old Sarah died, and Tom found himself unexpectedly heir to her shop and all its contents. (It was suggested by the street that he must have paid her for it during her lifetime in some way known only to himself and Sarah.) She had been a kind of unofficial pawnbroker, and her counter was concave from the bundles of pledges that had passed for forty years over the crumbling worm-eaten wood. The shop was very dirty. Teacups adhered irremovably to valuable Victorian *étagères*, stray cats sharpened their claws against the upholstery of a piece of Chippendale, dogs ate offal from dishes of Crown Derby. Dust, dead flies, the frail crisp carcases of spiders had accumulated in the window among the jumble of odd shoes and the sun-bleached garments of Green Street's dead. Tom and Mary cleaned and painted the shop, and opened it up as a green-grocery.

Mary contracted her husband's political views and dutifully echoed bitter things about blood iron and profits, or prophetic things about the coming struggle and throwing off the oppressor's yoke. She entered into the part eagerly enough, but if her husband had been a fascist or a monarchist she would have had no difficulty in espousing these causes with equal passion. She would rouse up her son in the middle of the night and talk to him of the spectre of unemployment, or would tearfully make him promise not to let her end her days in the work-house, which mysterious pledge the child wonderingly under-took, although, as he realized later, even by that time the workhouse had long been transformed into a maternity hospi-tal, gaily painted and surrounded by star-shaped flowerbeds planted with tulips or petunias according to the season. 'Re-member this, son,' his father would say in an admonitory voice, 'poverty isn't a crime.' But it was a vice, a habit Mary and Tom had contracted when they were young, and which they had retained, as some people retain for a lifetime an out-moded hairstyle or way of dress which were fashionable in their heyday. And just as the preservation of a thinning bun or a faded ringlet lends such people an illusion of perpetual youth, so Tom and Mary still lived on the threshold of the poorhouse, even when their possessions and style of living attested to the contrary. On Mondays they kept watch for the landlord who collected Ellen Youl's rent, and they held the same conversation about surrendering her hard-earned money to line the pockets of old Tysoe, a Shylock, a heartless and inhuman profiteer who'd never done a hand's turn of work in his life. He was a leech, a parasite, a usurer, a landlord, a word which Tom always whispered hoarsely, stressing both syllables and evoking a picture of incredible despotic arrogance and power, and it was always difficult to identify the word with the soft-spoken little man with the tooth-brush moustache and the vast yellowing herring-bone overcoat that reached the ground. But for all his apparent inoffensiveness he cut throats and battened on the poor, and extorted the widow's mite and sold his grandmother for twopence. Every week he entered 'eight-and-sixpence Paid' with a great convoluted capital P in the rent-book that Ellen Youl kept behind the clock, and then went away on a woman's bicycle. Mary would watch him ride away shakily down the street and pray that he might fall under the next bus, which would nevertheless have been too good a fate for the likes of him.

Poverty was a virtue beside which goodness and charity and kindliness and modesty were insignificant attributes. They were always wondering publicly where the next meal would come from, although there was never any real doubt while their cellar was stacked with cartons full of tinned foods. 'Just in case,' Tom said elliptically, in case of hardship, siege, war or revolution, which they expected at any moment like an overdue visit from an old friend or relative.

All the interesting and important things had either happened in the past or were going to happen in the future. 'The trouble with us,' Tom would say, 'is we're ahead of our time.' And he would sit back complacently in the greasy moquette armchair, and wait for time to catch up with him. In their speech the words 'Labour' and 'Tory' were synonyms for good and evil (or rather these words assumed the rôle of aetiological myth – good and evil were merely minor manifestations of these fundamental underlying principles of their cosmos). Mrs Raison's surliness, old man Arnold's lechery, even Mrs D.'s partiality to her Guinness, were mysteriously ascribed to Toryism, as if it were a more obscure and eighth deadly sin. Conversely, their own thrift, Mr Thigh's cheerfulness and Mr Travis's sobriety were evidence of 'Labour ways'. They were always talking about a better world for their children, and from earliest childhood their son had been woken up in the middle of the night and trundled through the streets in an ancient baby-carriage, and had been triumphantly held aloft by his parents in greeting to victorious Labour candidates in municipal by-elections, which for them always heralded the new order.

People were always coming to the house in the evening when the shop had closed. They littered the back parlour with tracts and leaflets and posters and slogans and improbably youthful photographs of ageing candidates. ('Your candidate speaks' as though announcing some secret and irresistible accomplishment.) On especially festive days they gathered around the piano and sang songs about the ennobling aspects of toil and messianic hymns about release from fetters and marching forth out of bondage. They stood in respectful silences in memory of martyrs and pioneers who had laid down their lives, and they paid tribute to their own martyr, Mrs Hindley, who had contracted pneumonia as she stood in the rain proclaiming her solidarity with a girl in a clothing factory who had been dismissed for calling the foreman an old bastard.

But their political enthusiasm only masked the poverty of their own relationship. One woman was not enough for Tom. On evenings when he wasn't attending meetings, he would dress up in his best navy-blue pinstripe suit, thread a carnation into his buttonhole, step into his fancy tan brogues and smooth down his hair with lard and sit for hours among the paper palms in the Winter Garden of the palatial roadhouse on the main route out of the town, where Ma B. led the singing every night. Mary saw her husband's sexual needs as a profound and considered insult against her. She spoke as if her husband had wilfully induced the demands of his own body to humiliate her. She did not love him herself, but she could not bear that he should be disloyal. 'Do not love me, but remain faithful' was her harsh injunction. She was prepared to subjugate her own revulsion and disaffection to her ideas of marital and family propriety, and expected him to do the same. And they believed they had been liberated from the superstition and self-abasement of the country as well as from the poverty and ignorance of the town. But they were not so easily released and the past held them like a jealous wife. They had selected each other without judgement or discrimination, simply because they had been thrown in each other's path. And they fled the truth of their incompatibility, and found refuge for a time in the belief that a change in the ownership of the means of production might even abolish Tom's sexual demands. For them marriage had nothing to do with personal needs, differing individual requirements. It was assumed that everybody was the same, and whenever anyone failed to find fulfilment in marriage – which occurred frequently – the other partner was automatically and unthinkingly rebuked as the source of all discord. Marriage meant a pledge of a lifetime of predictable behaviour, any deviation from which would be cited against the transgressor as proof of his or her wilful wickedness. As Tom was supplanted by the child in her affections, Mary found this the most natural thing in the world, while he was able to allege her growing coolness as the origin of his search for solace elsewhere. And they were both deluded. Their understanding of each other was impaired by all the fixed habits of thought and obligatory responses which they had inherited, and against which the reality of their lives beat vainly, like clenched and desperate fists on locked doors. They never realized that the poverty against which they fought had had far more corrosive effects upon their lives than the universal shortage of money.

She withdrew her support from his political activities, and he would sit alone listening mournfully to Moscow broadcasting to Europe and North America at four in the morning, Water Comes to Ashkhabad, violated air-space and over-fulfilment of quinquennial plans. Tom no longer appeared in the shop, but became a lorry driver, baker's roundsman, labourer, street-cleaner. He stayed away from home for long periods, and only visited the shop at intervals to help himself to money from the till. If his wife protested he hit her with anything that came to hand, and threatened to 'cut her to the brisket' if she interfered. A year or two later he returned to his family in Daventry, where he found work as a ratcatcher in farms, slaughterhouses and factories.

They were divorced – an enormity in our family, and a thing for which they had no ready response. They were inclined to be indulgent towards Mary, her husband's notoriety having absolved her from any suspicion of blame. There had to be an innocent and an injured party. (They worked indefatigably at forcing their experience into the bounds of the limited moral code which they claimed to live by. A cousin called Grace once allowed herself to be seduced by the master of the house where she worked as a maid. He provided her with money and clothes and paid for her daughter's education. The daughter grew up to a way of life which she could never have achieved without her mother's skilful manipulation of her lover, and as the years passed Grace came to attribute her seduction to an excess of motherly care about her child's future, although at the time she had been merely flattered and had enjoyed her employer's lovemaking. And since childhood was sacrosanct, and almost anything admissible in 'giving it the right start in life', she had no difficulty in creating the impression of a woman who had sacrificed everything for her daughter, who had yielded to the advances of a wild and sophisticated voluptuary – with what shrinking and heart-searching she alone knew – to prevent her daughter from becoming a poor skivvy like herself. (She wasn't in fact even a skivvy herself, but a most superior housemaid.) The breach of moral law was vindicated by the daughter's eager exploitation of the chances her mother had put at her disposal.)

As soon as Tom and Mary were separated, they bore each other no ill-will, and every Christmas he would appear in Green Street with a present of a goose in reparation for past wrongs, and a maudlin 'God bless you', and he was always given a glass of port and fifty cigarettes as a token of forgiveness. After some years of this custom, he evidently judged the cumulative expiatory effect of six annual geese sufficient to warrant suggestive remarks about not having known which side his bread was buttered, and pious wishes that he could have his time over again. He would linger over his port, doleful and woebegone, half expecting an invitation that never came to return from the exile which he had imposed upon himself. Like many of the men in our family, as his strength began to decline, he underwent a change of personality. The bluster and magniloquence gave way to a mild ingratiating desire to please. He grew unctuous and affable, but it was all attributed to cunning, an attempt to reinstate himself by making great display of his change of heart. During his last illness Mary relented, and had him transported from the disused railway carriage, in which he was then living, into the straw and blue fruit-wrapping paper and bones and specked oranges in the back parlour. He lived for three days.

7. Ritual

Aunt Ada and Uncle George always came on Christmas Eve.
They lived less than a mile away, but they always arrived
troubled and breathless, like people embarked upon a daring
and reckless adventure. They brought their luggage in brown-
paper parcels, as if they had been forced by rising flood-water
or an invading army to leave home without any prior warning.
Their stay created a sense of contrived spontaneity, of rehearsed makeshift. The whole house was disorganized, and as
a token of the importance of family congress, which could be
consummated only by a night spent under the same roof,
everybody slept in the greatest discomfort in arm-chairs and
camp-beds. Separation after the prolonged celebrations of
Christmas Eve would have been mutually more welcome and
more convenient, but the complete cycle of a whole day and
night spent in each other's company was considered to be an
inescapable necessity.

Their presence in the house caused the clock on the mantelpiece to move round to strange and fabulous hours, the every
existence of which had to be taken on trust in normal circumstances, for the whole family was generally in bed before ten
o'clock. But on this day of the year the fire was kept going all
night. On other days it was allowed to die down from eight
o'clock in the evening, and before anyone retired the embers
had to be raked through, and a sheet of corrugated iron placed
against the hearth as a preventive against the imagined in-
cendiary properties of dead ash. I was always fascinated by the
hands of the clock, open in an unaccustomed V at five to one –
time that meant daylight and movement in the street; and I
would move aside the curtain and marvel at the silence and
darkness outside, and the gaslight which lay like a liquid in the
still deserted road.

Ada and George didn't particularly enjoy Christmas any more than we did, but every year we submitted to George's reminiscences of all he did for his country in the Great War (he always emphasised its greatness as an implied contrast to weak and emasculate combats in which other people had taken part), and all for a shilling a day. His stories of encounters with Johnny Turk, or the screams of comrades who died in his arms after crude and improvized amputations of damaged limbs, he recounted not to illustrate the horror of war, but with a sense of perennial wonder that such unexampled and exotic things could have happened to anyone so humble as himself. The most harrowing of his tales concerned his attempt to climb a tree in order to wrench a German gun from the hand of a dismembered soldier, caught up in the branches after an explosion, and which he bore home as a trophy for his seven-year-old son. When George had finished – or sometimes before he had finished if he showed signs of going on too long – Ada would deliver her party pieces, or recall how she ought by right to have gone on the Halls, but had married George instead, and she jerked her thumb disparagingly and allowed the folly of her choice to speak for itself.

From the moment when the family assembled until they all departed two days later, they ate without remission. Eating was always for us a serious, even mournful rite. Most of our weekly income went on food. The branch of the family that 'got on' was always accused of having done so at the expense of their belly. Aunt Laura in Leicester, famous for her villa, managed to maintain it only by eating bread and lard at dinner time, and for this was much despised. 'Better by half pay a bread bill as a doctor's bill.' In our family you could never eat too much, and you were always urged to eat more and yet more, and if you suffered from lack of appetite, this was taken to be a deliberate and considered affront. When I took home people whose education or accent or customs mystified my mother, she would smile at them nervously, and, in order to assure them of her good will in spite of an inability to converse with them, would lavish cakes and biscuits upon them, and they would sometimes look upon her with astonishment, unable to understand the reason for her insistence when they had already expressed several times their lack of hunger.

At one time, perhaps when they were young, it is possible that endless games of cribbage and rummy and draw-the-well-dry, the sedate and doleful junketing, may have aroused great delight and amusement, but as the years go by Aunt Ada annoys everybody by never being able to remember what are trumps. Uncle George falls asleep over his beer, the children become restless and talk of going out – an unthinkable profanation of the act of self-worship which these family celebrations represented. Now there is a sense of weariness and lassitude, not simply in the physical process of ageing – although that is there too – but in the repetition of familiar prescribed actions performed now without convictions. Every year their enjoyment is more laboured. They are like sleepwalkers in the slow deliberate lifting of a wine-glass – as if it cost them every effort of which they were capable to raise it to their lips. George sprawls in a greasy chair, his feet in the hearth on a rag rug composed of still recognizable fragments of coats or trousers, with his false teeth in one hand and the other lying protectively over his genitals. Aunt tries to sing 'The Last Rose of Summer' as she has done for forty Christmases, but she is prevented from finishing by a fit of coughing and has to be given some brandy instead. In the kitchen my mother is washing up in the shallow yellow plaster sink with its fluted exterior and single brass coldwater tap discoloured by verdigris and rust. The beer is set down in a stone jug by the fire, and Uncle Bill automatically plunges a red-hot poker into the amber liquid, which used to delight us once with the sizzling ferment and vapour this produced. There are long silences under the bare electric light bulb suspended like a single drop of urine on its twisted flex. A fly settling on its surface casts a shadow big as a bird of prey upon the sprays of evergreen behind 'The Boy eating Cherries' and 'The Moneylenders being driven from the Temple'. The branches of dry dark laurel and holly, once symbols of the continuation of life even as the year died, now take on a new and ironical significance. But still no one doubts the necessity for the life they have always known. The established ceremony cannot be modified now, even though there may be something uneasy and self-conscious in its fulfilment.

After tea they would dredge up from memory tales that recorded the victory of the family over its enemies – a moment of triumph over the teacher who had a down on our Diane, Ellen's success in eliciting from a person an admission that the sinfulness of not sending her children to Sunday school was somewhat extenuated by their not having any shoes to go in, or Lill's 'rescue' of her cousin from the workhouse:

'My cousin Ada Mobbs, she was in the workhouse. Once a week I used to goo and have her out for the day. I'd take her out in the carrier's cart as fur as Earl's Barton. She was nearly blind and she had to scrub floors in the workhouse. They all wore a striped dress and a straw hat. Anyroad, there was this parson at Earl's Barton as took interest in Ada – because she was sharp, she had brains – and eventually he offered her a home. So I went and fetched her out one Wednesday like I always did, and then we took her to her new place and she changed into some proper clothes. I came back to Northampton in the carrier's cart, and I went dinxin' up to the workhouse and walked straight in and plonked her clothes on the counter and said, "I'm brought Ada Mobbs's things, she won't be needin' your hospitality any longer." They looked at me gone out; I reckon they thought I'd done her in.'

Most of these narratives were selected to confirm the family in its belief that it was in every way superior. It was irrepressible and feared no one, forthright, independent and uncommonly clever. They would often tell stories illustrating this which are claimed as their own by a thousand other families, as for instance the rejoinder to the parson who came collecting for the waifs and strays: 'If you lot wore your trousers the way you wear your collar there wouldn't be so many waifs and strays in the world.' Since they only told such things within the family they were never confronted or challenged by any of their other alleged originators. They were like any nation, tribe, clan or faction, singing and celebrating its triumphs, suppressing its reverses and defeats. Only occasionally they became bitter and spoke of failure or suffering, like the great-aunt who remembered her mother's references to a kinsman exiled in 'Van Demon's Land' for poaching. She said that whenever she had heard this as a child she had imagined it to be some subterranean hell, attended by fork-tailed devils and confused with the innumerable images of hell with which she had always been threatened by parents and teachers as part of their questionable attempts to discipline and control her. A few details of an ancient public hanging had long ago been committed to the collective memory of the family. As a child I seemed to catch the very smell of the gingerbread being sold outside the gaol on the spicy breath of the old men, who talked as if they had witnessed it, of children held aloft to get a better view of the spectacle, and the door in a blank wall twenty feet above the yard of the county gaol. 'They opened the door and he just walked through it, same as you might open the front door there and walk into the street, except there was no street for him to walk on. . . .'

Later in the evening they return to the songs, poems and hymns which have so deeply influenced their lives. Aunt Vi recites a poem taught her by some vague and rather suspect Brethren whose meetings she had been compelled to attend as a child. Although she learnt it when she was ten, she still declaims in a shrill posh aunts-and-uncles voice, like a perfectly remembered lesson, any forgetting of which would have been punished with the leather strap keeping up her father's trousers.

> Skylark, skylark, when you go up in the sky,
> Skylark, skylark, winging your flight so high,
> If among the angels mother you should see
> Ask her to come down again
> To poor daddy and me.

The respectful and melancholy silence which always followed this recitation indicated that it was regarded as an aesthetic experience of a high order. They had a large repertoire of affecting and improving songs of this kind, which all had to be gone through before the evening was over.

So the high-born child and the beggar
Passed heavenward side by side.
The ways of men are narrow
But the gates of heaven are wide.

(The only people from their own class who appeared in
these compositions were wastrels and drunkards who came to
a bad end or pious and sober artisans who had signed the
pledge of temperance and who behaved themselves lowly and
reverentially towards their betters. They were kept in their
place culturally as well as socially by a profound sense of their
own unworthiness, and even the generation after Vi and Ada,
who were brought up on the cinema, came to believe that real
passion and real emotion were inextricably and mysteriously
bound up with cocktails and leisure and exotic accents. Their
most uplifting experiences were provided by contact with
something remote and fabulous, *The Student Prince* or *The
Count of Luxemburg* on the end of a pier during their honey-
moon, and some cracked gramophone records of the Munn
and Felton Works Band playing extracts from *The Arcadians*
or *The Merry Widow*. They found their most elevating moment in the ninepennies of the Roxy Kinema, crying their eyes
out over *The Garden of Allah* or enchanted by the unspeakable
sophistication of pink feathers, gold lamé and ruched silk on
huge revolving Broadway stages. They always knew that their
own life didn't count. Real living could be done only by people
born to it. Their own emotions or sufferings were felt to
be of too little consequence to be of interest to anyone.
In this they followed the generation before them, Aunt
Maud who diligently followed the fortunes of the highest
in the land, and rejoiced and mourned at their births and
deaths with more conviction than she ever displayed when
anyone within her own family gave birth or died. When
divorces were announced among the nobility or gentry they
were held to be 'terrible tragedies', but when couples of her
own acquaintance separated they were stigmatized as 'loose-
livers'.)

Ada, as a consolation for her failure to appear on the halls –
which had been brought about by the intervention of her step-

mother – was allowed to perform on Christmas Eve for as long
as she chose.

> O the snow, the beautiful snow,
> How the flakes gather and laugh as they go!
> Whirling about in its maddening fun,
> It plays in its glee with everyone!
>
> Once I was as pure as the snow, but I fell,
> Fell like the snowflakes from heaven to hell.
> Fell to be spat on, trampled and beat,
> Fell to be trampled like filth in the street.
> But God in the stream that for sinners doth flow
> Washed me, and I shall be whiter than snow!
>
> Out in the cold and blinding sleet,
> Out in the cold and dreary street;
> No place of shelter, no place to go,
> No mother to guide him, in her grave she lay low,
> Cast out on this wide world was poor little Joe.

She would recite 'Papa's Letter', and sing 'Darling, I am Growing Old' and 'Bird in a Gilded Cage' and a song about what
folly it is to build costly mansions on sin's delusive sand. Often
these commonplace poems and songs, which they thought
poignant and edifying, became vehicles for their own suffering,
and sometimes Aunt Ada would invest 'Skylark' with a fervour and meaning which the words did not merit. All her
anguish and unhappiness came through in the contorted face
and choking tears, independently of the content of the song. In
spite of the triteness of the sentiment, it was elevated by the
intensity of genuine feeling that she infused into it. It was sad
that such intensity should have to struggle through these mean
and unworthy compositions before it could find expression.

So it was with their speech. They poured all their own living
emotions and feelings into universal set phrases and locutions.
They never pierced the shroud of language which passed from
generation to generation, which smothered and stifled their
own experience, and rendered indistinguishable their grief or
their joy or their suffering from anybody else's.

In this way even their pleasures followed a set formal

pattern, a slow somnambulistic *pavan*, every movement
of which had been determined at some time outside living
memory. At the important moments of their life, at a birth,
and especially after a death, conversation took the form of
a sepulchral and stylized chorus. After Ellen's funeral they
met in the front parlour and performed a lament for the dead
woman.

'Well ... There's another one laid to rest.'

'Still, she was a good age.'

'She'd had her life, and she was a good woman.'

'Aah, she'd a-bin eighty-seven a-Friday.'

'It's sad to see 'em goo though.'

'What sort of end did she 'ave? Was she quiet?'

'Shh, she's a bit overwrought, duck, let 'er alone.'

'Well, you're bound to be.'

'Anyway, it was a lovely funeral.'

'It was what she would a-wanned.'

'Not a lot o' fuss.'

'I'm never seen the street so quiet.'

'Only the Barker woman's curtains not drawn.'

'And she's only ninepence in the shillin'.'

'What sort of a stone was you gunner get?'

'When air Floss died we 'ad black marble. And a Nangel
'oldin' up a book as said, "The Lord 'ath given and the Lord
'ath took away." '

'We 'ad some green chips for air Dad, ever so reasonable at
the Co-op.'

'No, we ain't 'avin' nothin' o' that ... Just a vorse wi'
Mother on it. Cemetery's cluttered up enough as it is.'

'Well, they're gotter put yer somewhere.'

'Oughder be burnt. Everybody. I know one thing – I shall be
cremated when I goo.'

'Oo no ... 'Tain't right ... You 'ave to be buried ... If they
do ... resurrect yer like it says in the Bible on the Day o'
Judgement you're gunner be in a bad way if there ain't nothin'
left but 'eap of ash, ain't yer?'

'I don't want resurrectin', duck, they can leave me be. When
I get rid o' my body I 'ope to Christ I never see the bloody

thing agen, the trouble an' pain it's gev me. . . .'

'That's a terrible thing to say, Lill. If I thought all I'd bin
through was only so's I should be pushin' up the daisies when
I'm gone . . . well – I'd give up the ghost 'ere an' now. . . .'

'Well, sittin' 'ere ain't gunner get the baby a noo frock.'

'Don't let it get yer down, duck.'

'You don't 'ave to, do yer?'

Even when the ancient country superstitions and rites finally
died, they were supplanted by ceremonies just as stringent as
those which they replaced. Half a lifetime's savings could be
expended on 'doing things properly' for a wedding or funeral,
and unless the event were invested with sufficient ostentation,
it was thought to be incomplete, an insult to those newly married or just buried. The family were at pains to convince themselves of the universal significance of everything that happened
to them, in spite of the evidence which every day provided of
the indifference of other people. The ceremonial was a public
assertion of the gravity of occurrences which to those not involved in them might seem unremarkable or commonplace.

8. Speech

Just as all conversations followed an inevitable and predictable course, so the words, phrases and expressions which they comprised were determined by the same irresistible sense of necessity. (How these conversations ever came to be initiated is unknown. By the time they reached the ears of anyone now living, they were so deeply impressed upon family memory, and were uttered with such authority, that any violation or alteration of them would have been as unthinkable as an amendment to a hallowed formulary, or an unexpected irreverent response in a litany or catechism. Those who first gave voice to the ideas and feelings embodied in such conversations must have had a daring unequalled for many generations. When any new event occurred that could not fail to be incorporated into their dialogues a marriage or a death, some particularly praiseworthy or reprehensible piece of conduct – it had to be quoted in support of their view of the world. What they never did was modify their view in the light of such new events or experience. They were like the guardians of a sacred revealed truth, and anything that might have undermined its universal validity had to be adapted or amended until it could work no harm against what was for them an established and inviolable reality.)

The identity of idiom obscured individual characteristics more effectively than any other aspect of their lives. Nobody developed an independent, personal way of speaking. They shared a tongue assimilated uncritically from the past. Everything spoke of their origin; the idioms borrowed from obsolete crafts and occupations of the countryside ('tup-reddle' for lipstick; 'She looks like a sow with sidepockets', said of a woman unnecessarily adorned); expressions connected with the weather and the passage of the seasons ('You come like snow in harvest' would be the greeting to an unexpected and un-welcome visitor); vegetable or animal life ('It's a poor hen as can't scrat for one chick,' said of a woman with only one child who complains that she is unable to manage it; 'It's a sign of a hard winter when the hay starts to run after the horse,' refer-ring to a girl who reverses the conventional process of court-ship by openly and shamelessly setting her cap at the man). Some of the ideas preserved in these expressions would have been forgotten long ago if they had not become congealed in stock sayings and proverbs. 'He's got ears like a rabbit.' The awareness of the rabbit's highly developed sense of hearing would have faded but for the unthinking comparison which perpetuated it.

Like popular speech in any tongue their idiom had at its core many images and similes taken from the human body and its functions, and often of great crudity and immediacy. 'She looks at him as if the sun shone out of his arse' was a pejora-tive and disapproving reference to anyone so immoderately preoccupied with a lover that she had no time for anyone else. Whenever Ellen's children were forced to stay indoors on a rainy day so that they fretted and wandered impatiently from room to room, asking her what they could do, she would sometimes reply in exasperation, 'Oo shit and fall back in it,' and if her daughter complained of having nothing to wear she would say, 'Black your behind and goo naked.'

There remained a number of words that were unaltered Anglo-Saxon. Ellen, smoothing out her pinafore, would say, 'It's as good as noo, it'll last me my time, there ain't a *brack* in it' (A S bracean, to break). Of a day of alternating showers and sun they would say, 'They're treacherous, these *glaudy*-mornings, I wouldn't go out without a coat' (A S glafan, glawan). Speaking of her son Ellen often declared, 'The trouble with our Joe he won't stick at one thing, he will allus do things be dribs and *drabs*' (A S drabbe, dregs). Every day they used set phrases of great antiquity, often suggestive of early English poetry: it was always the proud claim of our family that we 'didn't meddle nor make with other folks', and our speech was full of similar alliterative phrases – 'chop and change', 'fret and fume', 'weep and wail', 'rant and rave'. There were many rhyming phrases: 'We don't want other people in our house, peering and leering about', 'They're allus moanin' and groanin' about sommat or other', and a number of archaic and poetical words frozen in set phrases that would otherwise never pass our lips. 'Time out o' mind' (meaning memory), 'mop and mow'. In almost every sentence would occur a saying or locution that bore witness to an earlier and not completely superseded tongue. If children complained of not feeling hungry and refused to eat, their parents would say, 'It's no wonder, all them *mullocks* you're bin eatin' – a word familiar to Chaucer:

> The mullocke on an hepe yswepid was
> And on the floor ycast was a canvas;
> And all this mullocke in a sive ithrowe,
> And sifted and ipluckid many a throwe ...
> *'Chanon's Yeman's Tale'*

But they quite simply knew no other word in this context. They still used a number of Shakespearean words. When Edwin Youl threatened to 'jowl' his children's heads against the wall, he echoed Hamlet, 'How the knave jowls it to the ground...' Much of their language had remained intact for centuries, just as some of their ideas – possibly those concerned with kinship and family duty – must have persisted from a similar period.

They were constantly placing sayings and proverbs, summoned forth by every occasion and event as the only possible response, and often prefaced by 'When all's said and done' or 'Well, you know what they say', which was probably intended as further evidence of its authenticity and validity. Their speech was full of grave and sententious utterances, quoted with finality, as though the wisdom they resumed were a worthy and adequate comment on situations of the greatest complexity. Whenever anyone suggested that he felt sorry for Vera or Dopey Freda, they would shake their head sagely and declare, 'Aah. Pity without relief is like mustard without beef.'

If a neighbour came in to borrow something she would be sent away with less than half the quantity of whatever commodity she needed and the admonition 'Oo guz a-borrerin', guz a-sorrerin'.

Allusive sayings abounded in all their speech. Of a woman who disapproved of other people's sexual success, they would say, 'It's easy enough to hold the latch down when nobody's trying to get in.' If anyone called at the house in Green Street to see Edwin Youl and, finding him away from home, tried to leave a message with his wife, she would raise her hand in protest and cut him off: 'There ain't no sense in trying to plough with the heifer.' Anyone who talked too much would be told that he had too much of what the cat licks its arse with. If in conversation Edwin Youl was appealed to by his wife for confirmation of some view or opinion (which had probably emanated from him, anyway), and if he responded with his customary ungraciousness, she would retort, 'What can you expect from a pig but a grunt?' An interfering neighbour would be told to sweep up her own doorstep before she started on other people's, and if anyone met with failure in an undertaking he would say, 'That's all right, there's more than one way of killing the cat.' Those who boasted of their sexual adventures were said to be 'crying roast meat', and if anyone were offered a drink late at night she would say, 'I shall be peeing like a fat wench all night.' It was as though they believed that meaning could be more effectively conveyed by avoiding too much accuracy, and by relying instead upon suggestion and indirect reference.

They spoke with great economy of language. Nothing was ever said for the sake of speaking, nothing added to impress or to excite admiration. They never trusted articulate people, and always held 'the gift of the gab' in great contempt. Long silences supervened in all their conversations, and verbal exchanges seemed to be a weak substitute for some secret means of communication which they took care to conceal from outside observers. They had many evasive answers for those who asked indiscreet questions. They were guarded in all replies, unwilling to disclose to anyone – even to members of their own family – more than a minimum about themselves and their own lives. If anyone asked them how much something had cost the stern and uncommunicative reply would be 'Money and fair words'. Curiosity about the purpose of an errand would be met with invariable unsmiling rebuff 'To see a man about a dog', and the question 'When?' provoked the retort 'Oo some day, or never at the farthest'. When S. left his wife and the children asked where he was, the only information their mother offered was 'Two fields the other side China'. They were reluctant to give praise. If a daughter asked how she looked before going out the highest compliment she could expect would be 'You'll pass in a crowd with a good push'. If there had been a misunderstanding, and someone tried to explain his mistaken point of view by saying 'O I thought . . .', he would be interrupted by 'You shouldn't think, not till the crows build in your bum, then you should start wondering how they got the sticks there', and the kindest thing they could find to say of Dopey Freda was that she would never make the lads sigh at their suppers.

As they talked of the *slommakin* neighbours *glinting* at you from behind the curtains, the *mardy*-arsed children and the *blarting* women having a *tune* (crying) over nothing, Vera *gawning* around (A S ginian, to yawn) as if she wasn't sharp, the smoke *puthering* out from the grate when the wind blew down the chimneys, the old man *golloping* his food, Gran *scratting* about like a blue-arsed fly, the kids *yawping* and *grizzling* in the *jitties*, the sister who *takes tut* over nothing, people *flacking* in and out of the house all day long, the roads all *claggy* with mud, the *shutting-in* of the day (which on their lips meant twilight), it was possible to imagine a vigorous and independent dialect, but none of it was of recent evolution. The force and meaning of once living images had been weakened and muted by the prolonged transmission from generation to generation. They were spoken without thought of the original acts and occasions that had given them birth. The fragments of poetry enshrined in their language were preserved unwittingly – when as Ellen remembered the 'gret gipsy-legged girls' of her youth, or accused her children of being 'cow-tongued', rough one side and smooth the other, deceitful. Similarly, when Edwin Youl said to his wife that he was sick and tired of her and was going to bed to get some peace, and she replied that the only peace she could look forward to would be when they put him to bed with a shovel, she was being neither as inventive nor as cruel as this remark may have seemed to anyone hearing it for the first time. It was an accepted exchange, like his response to her when she told him to shut her mouth, 'Well, you'll never shut your'n till you get the bugger full o' mould.'

Most of their ideas had persisted in the same way. Ideas dwelt in the received language as easily and naturally as birds inhabited the sky, and all the facile wisdom – 'It's a long lane as has no turning' when they were unhappy, 'Oo you'll live till you die' said to anyone who complained of any trifling ailment, 'There's nothing done without trouble but letting the fire out' to someone confronted by a difficult undertaking – was never questioned simply because it existed already, and this lent it universal authority and meaning. They felt the acquired idiom to be adequate for all they could possibly need to say; or it may be that unfamiliarity with any other words led them to the belief that nothing else existed.

They were so profoundly imbued with the retrenched vocabulary, the idioms and sayings, even the sentence-constructions, that anyone who did not share the same speech was immediately recognisable. A single word that was too long, a genteel inflexion, an unaccustomed comparison, and the person who uttered them was betrayed. They could not allow that people adopted another linguistic usage for any other reason than snobbery. It was assumed that theirs was the only natural speech, and everything else was affectation. In this way, even people of good will who sought to make contact were rebuffed. A schoolteacher, anxious to persuade parents of the usefulness and advantages of a child's staying at school for an extra year, would find himself treated with hostility and suspicion because of his alien non-communicating idiom, as though he wanted to retain the child under his tutelage for some unfathomable and nefarious end not revealed to the parents. One of the family's children, who showed great ingenuity in inducing illnesses to escape the compulsory netball which she loathed, was once called a 'sham' by her teacher. Her mother was infuriated by the application of this word to her daughter (partly, she admitted, because she wasn't quite sure what it meant), and she threatened the offending schoolmistress with physical assault if she ever used such expressions in connection with her daughter again. 'You needn't talk posh with me,' she cried at the puzzled woman, who protested that it was essential to maintain a strong disciplinary hand if the nation's children were to grow up into decent citizens instead of riff-raff and hooligans, using in her turn the only idiom she had at her command.

The greatest criticism of the way they spoke is not that it was inaccurate. (Indeed, some of their words and vowel-sounds were vindicated by the traditional Anglian speech of Mercia, which preceded by many hundreds of years anything resembling standard English.) Its greatest disadvantage was that it stifled the personality and denied individual expression, and made of every aspect of their life a bitter and inescapable subjection.

The language altered little with the immediate change from country to town. It took several generations for the Anglo-Saxon words relating to their craft to fall into oblivion. (Some of our family had been thatchers, or *thackers* as they called themselves, and they continued to use words like *yelm* for straw, *dike* for ditch; they retained the pronunciation of *ship* for sheep (A S scip), *wic* for week (A S wicu), *nem* for name, *hus* for house, *ett* for eat.) They learned one way of speaking which they could not alter, and a single accent which they were unable to modify. It is only in the last generation that the once impregnable idiom has been fractured and broken, and the old find themselves suddenly speaking an unintelligible tongue. All at once the stylized ritual phrases, the mummified images, the fixed inflexions and cadences are full of a plaintive lamenting music. The old are aware of an inability to make themselves understood, even to their own children, and they realize that they will be the last ones to use the dialect. Their children are ashamed, and mock it, but although they eliminate it from their own speech, they do at least still hear it. When their children die, even a passive consciousness of the dialect will disappear. The language, like the ideas and beliefs of the past, is in a state of rapid deliquescence. It may well yield to greater diversity and fluidity, but this does not lessen the pain of its passing among those who have known nothing else.

9. Work

There was neither dignity nor self-fulfilment in their labour, in spite of the frequent sermons and exhortations to which they were exposed and which exalted the sanctity of toil and the salubrity of industry. They were directed into occupations that corresponded neither to their abilities nor to their preferences. None of the memories that survive of the generations who worked in the fields suggests a joyful and harmonious oneness with the soil. The old couple who reaped half an acre of corn on their wedding day were only one generation removed from those who spent their childhood in the fields around Long Buckby in the eighteen-thirties, scaring the crows and picking stones. The stories which survive from this period evoke a brutalized and ignorant peasantry, eating rooks and starlings, burning breadcrumbs and infusing them in boiling water to simulate tea, awaiting the weekly visit of the relieving officer or the hearse from the workhouse or infirmary. Some of the family's women made lace, either on their front doorsteps or sitting by night with a solitary candle placed in a wooden stool surrounded by three glass globes filled with water which magnified the light, as they placed their pins on the hard-worn cushion, jangling their bobbins and passing on the mournful and desolate vision which has devolved upon all members of the family as effectively as a hereditary curse.

Some of those who were in service are inclined to linger regretfully on wedding feasts and hunting parties of legendary splendour, but their nostalgia does not redeem the terror of the eleven-year-old girl who was transported one cold February day in a carrier's cart to live in an attic eighty miles away from home, or the weariness of the woman who spent half a lifetime cleaning corridors, the ends of which were invisible through the mist. If Tom F. still boasts that his employer 'knew all of us by name' (as though to retain the names of thirty people stretched human memory to its farthest limits), this scarcely compensates the loneliness of Daisy G., a lady's maid who died on Christmas Day, and whose employer gave voice to no more charitable a sentiment than 'How tiresome of her to die on Christmas Day', and who sent immediate word to her kinsfolk to remove her corpse from the premises at once.

There were few in our family who took pride in their work, or who had cause to. Uncle Charlie, a thatcher many years retired, is a rare exception. 'I were out fifty years in all weathers, an' if I 'ad a wik on the club it were as much as I did 'ave ... Me an' ole Sam Underwood ... What 'e didn't know about thackin' warn't wuth knowin' ... Past master 'e were ... "Come on, boy," 'e used to say, "let's 'ave another stelch on." I can see 'im now atop o' the ladder – gret 'ands 'e'd got on 'im, one of 'is'n'd mek two o' mine ... Aah, and U'm felt 'em aside me ear'ole many a time 'cause I couldn't get the 'ang o' the yelmin' when I fust started ... An' 'e used to bed 'is eaves in 'andsome. ...'

But even this slight satisfaction was denied to most of those who worked in the boot and shoe industry. Few of them were skilled enough to find much delight in the transformation of the unyielding acrid-smelling animal hides into footwear. The smell from the tanneries filled every street, it permeated the hair and clothing and even clung to the flesh of those who worked there. Edwin Youl had been a clicker (he cut the uppers of the shoes from the hide) and it was always his boast that he could 'cut a skin so's there ain't a piece left big enough to make a bootlace'; but for most of the other men it was a question of a rented workshop, shared with two or three other single men, who worked, ate and slept in one room.

Until the end of the last century most of the work was collected from the master shoemakers or clickers and then taken home to underground kitchen workshops, lean-to sheds or bedrooms that projected into the yard at the back of every house. Every Monday the workers went to pick up the week's supply, and some of them, always eager to introduce cere-

monial into their lives, even dressed up for the occasion in a
top-hat and frock-coat, often mouldy with age, but which they
reserved solely for 'going to shop'. Accoutred in this way, they
imagined their chances of obtaining a share of the often scant
work vastly enhanced. Saturday was the busiest day. Work was
then submitted, pay tickets made up, and consequently no
work was given out on that day. It was assumed that nobody
worked on the Sabbath, and people would listen attentively for
sounds of surreptitious tapping issuing from their neighbours'
houses, and if any such could be distinguished the offenders
would be roused up and called to account, less in protest
against profanation of that holy day than against the unfair
advantage they might acquire by working during a period of
general repose. On Monday, therefore, there was always a long
queue for work, and it was sometimes late in the day before
the last workman was served. Those low on the list were ex-
horted by their wives to mend the footwear of their own
household or to sharpen their kit, but more often they made
their way to 'The Garibaldi' where they 'boozed all day for a
shilling', having little incentive to return home to the kitchen,
awash from an overflowing copper, with steam discolouring the
paint as it condensed and fell in long shiny streaks down the
wall, and not relishing the cold stringy meat and dried peas
and rice pudding that invariably made up Monday's dinner.

As the machinery became complex more factories became
established, and few people continued outworking after the
turn of the century. All the children of Ellen Youl began work
in one of those early factories, and of this novelty and privilege they still bear the marks today – backs so bent that as they
shuffle along the road on their way to collect a quarter of
margarine and a bundle of sticks all they can see is the pavement beneath them, the single remaining example of the once
ubiquitous head-turban covering Aunt Lou's baldness, which
resulted from some unguarded machinery in the factory where
she worked at the age of twenty.

The employment of children as human scarecrows, the
necessity of serving imperious and ungrateful gentlefolk as
maids and gardeners did not bring them any more satisfaction

than sorting pairs of shoes or glueing wisps of nylon hair on to the heads of plastic dolls. I cannot imagine anyone wanting to perpetuate proletarian culture. The conditions that created it were a cruel bondage which mutilated and destroyed, and those who would prolong it – even in the name of some prospective and possibly beneficial revolution – would need the ruthlessness and inhumanity of a circus owner who breeds a race of dwarfs from some dishonourable motive of personal gain. The release is not painless: not all the inhabitants of occupied cities throw themselves into the arms of their liberators. We were imbued with too many ancient beliefs, our lives were impregnated with too many customs for them to be repudiated without the bitterest feeling of loss and regret. But we had been as effectively deprived of freedom as if we had been physically confined. The absolute and unquestioned morality prevented us from taking the responsibility for our own lives; our preconceived demands and expectations of other people did not allow us to accept what they might have had to offer. Puzzled that happiness did not necessarily follow unwavering commitment and constant allusion to the sacred idea of family and kinship, they could reach one another only by inflicting pain, all the mothers cheated of the limitless love that their idea of 'motherhood' told them should flow towards them in an unending stream, all the wives uncherished after a few years of marriage, denouncing their consorts for their inconstancy, all the members of the family who attributed their unsatisfied longings and unrequited affections to the failings and shortcomings of others.

10. Liberation

Of course some members of the family had emancipated themselves in the past. Aunt Laura was the archetype of escape
through the interest of her employers, and that was in the
eighteen-eighties. When she came to be treated with more kindliness and liberality than a parlourmaid had any right to expect, the family at first felt vicariously gratified, but as it became clear that she was being encouraged to acquire alien
characteristics and pretensions, family feeling turned against
her. It was even suggested that at the age of fourteen she had
been the object of the wealthy boot manufacturer's attentions,
not for her intelligence, but because of her pale skin and black
braided hair. Some went so far as to assert that he had seduced
her, and her older brothers were all for going to Leicester and
confronting the monster with his imagined crime. Although
the girl was closely questioned before a family tribunal and no
suggestion was elicited of any impropriety committed against
her, they were not wholly convinced that the evil-doer had not
robbed her even of the ability to answer truthfully the oblique
and awkward interrogation to which she was subjected. For all
they knew all boot manufacturers might have been ravishers of
children. Presently the odium that his putative crime had
earned him was transferred to the willing recipient of his fav-
ours. She was accused of 'not knowing where her arse hung',
of getting too high in the instep.

Her eager renunciation of their values must have hurt them
cruelly, and they had to justify themselves against her success,
although at the same time the pride in her achievement ling-
ered. The imperious announcement that one of her increasingly rare visits was imminent would cause a frenzy of scour-
ing and scrubbing and washing, of which Laura always seemed

quite unheedful as she sat briefly on the horsehair sofa and sipped tea from the side of the cup which nobody else used. Once her chilling presence had removed itself, however, she became once more an object of veneration and respect. The children in Green Street were taught to speak of the sumptuousness of her dwelling with its ornamental commodes and chiffoniers and mahogany cheval-glasses. The ambiguous attitude towards Aunt Laura finds its counterpart today in that of all the mothers whose children receive a better education than their parents enjoyed. The public boast that 'they make proper little gentlemen of 'em at the Grammar School' often conceals shame and perplexity when the proper little gentlemen return home, impatient and critical of the way their parents live. They marvel at the remote and inaccessible places in which their children's minds move, and as they leaf timidly through a book left on the kitchen table they wonder who this Go-eth can be and whether it is he who is responsible for their son's alienation.

Whenever Laura's achievement was spoken of, it was sure to be followed by an instance of failure in the same undertaking, and the scapegoat in their admonitory examples was generally a cousin called Irene, who had once had a brief and predictable relationship with a doctor's son. The family had entreated her to 'stick to her own sort', and not to 'play with fire', but she had paid them no heed, and had accordingly been left high and dry and pregnant. During the time of the liaison she had scorned the qualms and the apprehensions of her relatives. He had left her 'to go away to college', a chimerical place into which they could never have hoped to pursue him in search of reparations. In spite of her earlier haughtiness, the family were magnanimous enough to receive the spurned and shamed girl again among themselves, if only as living proof of their own forbearance and of the folly of trying to escape like a refugee from one's lawful country. . . .

There would probably have been many other apostates from the family and the way of life it represented if the opportunity had existed. The few renegades were pursued so vengefully and unremittingly that it was impossible not to be aware of an underlying hypocrisy and envy in the universal condemnation of the middle-class values which they had embraced. The self-assertion of the women in 'The Garibaldi' was always uncertain and defensive in spite of its apparently clamorous blatancy; and the streets were always something provisional and impermanent – a pause, a resting-place in a long unbroken journey.

The family had always maintained its fundamental isolationism and withdrawal from others, and the grudging fellowship of the streets was something forced upon them by circumstances, to which they submitted unwillingly, rancorous and ungracious beneath the acts of friendship which they were compelled to perform. They were always jealous and emulous, and anxious to preserve their lives against the encroachments of others. They took an exaggerated pride in their property (even when it belonged to someone else), the tireless old women who were never still, scrubbing the cracked and pitted flags, hanging strips of dusty coconut matting out of the window, throwing sour-smelling soapy blankets over the clothes-line in the backyard, polishing the letterbox through which nothing ever came but a coal bill and an occasional uninformative letter from a daughter in America.

The children, too, became objects of rivalry and envy. If a neighbour's child appeared with a new ribbon in her hair, a pair of boots or a bonnet had to be got hold of somehow, and the puzzled and reluctant child of the family, bedizened with the new article, would be thrust triumphantly into the street, where its splendour eclipsed that of the pert and presumptuous neighbour's child, and caused the smile of exultation to fade as she ran home to her mother. And she would not appear again until another ornament had been acquired that could restore her to the pre-eminence she had so briefly enjoyed. The children were bewildered counters in a game they did not understand. Whenever two mothers met by chance in the street, each would launch immediately into a eulogy upon her own child's intelligence, success or beauty, and if she were interrupted by the other one, engaged upon a similar encomium, she managed to hear only those parts of it that reminded her of some out-

standing feature in her own offspring which she had overlooked, and which gave her an excuse to interrupt in her turn.
It was all very well to offer an encouraging smile to the cripple
in his leg-irons, or to the girl who sat mysteriously 'wasting
away' on the doorstep, for we knew quite well that they
offered no threat to us and our own children. We could afford
to be magnanimous as far as they were concerned, but those
who were sound and healthy were constantly disparaged, their
accomplishments belittled, their intelligence declared to be of a
mediocre order.

Although we might vilify those who lived in material ease,
and feign to despise the great houses which stood in isolation
and at rare intervals along the main road with their stained-
glass and conservatories full of gilded wicker-chairs and plum-
coloured plush and vases of tall bleached grasses, their Rapun-
zel-towers and turrets, their inscriptions – *Rheinfelden* or
Santa Lucia – carved in Gothic characters in blocks of sand-
stone, and their laurel-bordered drives leading to the orna-
mented outhouses for carriages, our attitude towards the house
which the family had been unlawfully deprived of and the
acerbity with which we always spoke of the usurpers of our
property did not suggest the indifference we professed. Indeed,
as time went by and the actual memory of the seizure became
fainter, the narration of it had to be renewed with fresh
supplementary detail and an embellishment in order to maintain a just degree of anger and vexation among those who
heard it and for whom it no longer had any immediacy. In the
original story, the illegitimacy of Ellen Youl, the legatee of
Son Lyman's will, was said to have come to light fortuitously,
but in later years the disclosure of this fact came to be a calculated malevolent action on the part of her brother Gus.

While we were poor poverty was virtuous, and we never
failed to announce our solidarity with the poor, but as it began
to decline it changed slowly into a sign of shiftlessness and
irresponsibility. And now that we are no longer poor we have
ceased to disguise our profound indifference towards other
people. We know that we shall never need their help again,
and even the pretence of neighbourliness and concern for them

has been abandoned. The already tenuous bonds linking them to us have been loosed still further by our new-found pre-occupation with material possessions – which is not the sad elegiac affection of an old woman for a pair of long-necked wrought-iron vases that have been in her family for three generations, not the feeling for the carefully dusted row of school prizes – *With Kitchener in Khartoum, The Brave Men of Eyam* – with their gleaming gilt-edged pages which testify to an intelligence that was never allowed to flower, not the sentimental pride of old T. in the tarnished brass bedstead to which, he recalls, he brought his wife on their wedding night fifty years ago, treasures so laboriously acquired that were really treasures, meaningfully connected as they were with human relationships, but an aimless and rapacious amassing of goods which have no significance beyond themselves. And the liberation – which should have been a triumphant and jubilant discovery that human beings are capable of exerting a positive and decisive influence upon the course and conduct of their own lives instead of yielding passively to forces supposedly beyond their control, has taken on the aspect of a new and joyless subjection. Now they are dominated by their posses-sions – a natural consequence of the earlier mistrust and sus-picion of other people, whom they never learned to deal with adequately and who have never been anything but potential rivals and competitors for too little work or food or even affec-tion. And they are puzzled by the lack of plenitude in their lives which frequently accompanies their economic independ-ence. The family has been fragmented into far smaller units and the great web of kinship has been destroyed. They have come to realize how little they have in common and have separated. They are like people at the end of a long journey who, about to be reunited with those they love, are made aware of the imperfections and inadequacies of their travelling com-panions who, however, had been welcome enough during the period of their exile and isolation.

11. Collapse

The street is condemned now, and the wind blows through the derelict houses. Strips of corrugated iron beat against the window-frames, a zinc bath scrapes the wall on its rusty nail. The white china doorhandles are smashed, the fragile gas-mantles flaking into a fine powder, the blue tin advertisements outside the corner shops corroded by rust, advertisements for products no longer on sale – cough-cures and cordials and remedies for indigestion, forgotten now like the people they killed or cured. A chipped enamel plaque proclaims the New Palace of Varieties, a grand array of talent at popular prices and a change of programme every night. The boards at the windows of Mrs Hurry's Beds for Working Men and the great ceremonially laid yellow stones at the base of a Methodist chapel are defaced by the carvings of children, and the rain has not washed away all the hopscotch and London-to-York games and the loves of ten-year-olds chalked on the uneven pavement.

Everything has been left as it stood. A dead bird lies in its cage in the window, a dusty tray of butterflies impaled on pins hangs obliquely on a parlour wall, milk bottles in congealed cream rings stand on the scrubbed deal tables. Some shreds of blue velvet curtain still screen the narrow staircase, and the paper chrysanthemums, bought by a grandmother in fear of a gipsy's curse, collect the dust in great glazed china pots. The broken springs and black wet horsehair protrude like a monstrous pubescence from the belly of a discarded leather sofa, and some grass is growing out of the back of a clock stopped at twenty to four. In the back rooms upstairs there lingers the acrid smell of animal hides. Strips of tarnished leather, a rusty awl and peeling iron last are strewn across a broken wooden work-bench. There is a hole in the wall where the ornamental H of a shoescraper stood, a deep groove is worn in the crumbling doorstep, and the window-sills have been eroded by the handlebars of bicycles. A thin drizzle smears the cobbles and the dead leaves spiral through the unhinged doors and along the dark passageways with their brown waxed-paper dado. In one of the houses two people shelter from the weather, but in the others nothing disturbs the rats chewing Nan and Pap as they sat one fair afternoon long ago on the back doorstep, brown and faded and still smiling. A thread of decorative blue brick stands out against the red, announces Industrial Dwellings 1860.

In each interior the abandoned belongings remain like those of refugees overtaken by sudden disaster; a stained striped flock mattress, fragments of rosy china vases and teapots and Coronation mugs of five reigns, blue-eyed Victorian Jesuses in gilt frames suffering the little children to come unto them, a Monarch of the Glen, school prizes awarded to the names of old men and women for Diligent Study and Application – *Isabel's Secret* or *A Sister's Love*, stories abounding in hospices and orphans and untimely deaths and little girls in frilly pinafores taking the place of Mamas who'd been called Home, serious and stoical at eight years old. *Joy's Jubilee, the Story of how a Little Girl spent the Jubilee of our Beloved Queen.* Smudged letters from close relatives in distant countries sympathizing in a bereavement and wishing they could be near at such a time, some great wrought-iron vases bequeathed to her children by a suspicious mother who doubted their ability to remember her without some huge and material token that she had indeed existed. A few torn pages from a collection of Sacred Songs:

> But I've been adopted, my name's written down,
> The heir to a mansion, a robe and a crown;
> A tent or a cottage – why should I care?
> They're building a palace for me over there!

It is as if they had woken one day and realized that all the possessions their families had so long cherished were suddenly without meaning or value for them, and in order to proclaim their emancipation from the past had simply abandoned all the objects associated with life in these streets. Nothing evokes more powerfully those who lived here than the discarded belongings which were once inseparable from them – Vera, with her thin black hair cropped short as a boy's, standing on the doorstep and talking to the empty street about the noises in her head; Hilda, a child of thirty-five, playing hopscotch by herself and chanting:

> Cowlady, cowlady, fly away home,
> Your house is on fire, your children at home.
> There's only one left and that's Ann,
> And she crept under the frying-pan. . . .

the old men toiling home from the allotment on a boneshaker of a bicycle, a spring cabbage or a stick of rhubarb under their arm, home to the epitaph-quoting old women with their grave-yard cough and dislocated walk and swollen legs and their hope that in spite of everything they may yet 'gather at the river where the angel-feet have trod. . . .', Granny Bray reading births and deaths and frosts and strangers in the house from the embers in the grate, Mrs P.'s efforts to get her daughter to church before she fell to bits, Ma Barcock with her drawers round her ankles, peeing in the gutter outside 'The Garibaldi' and singing 'California Here I Come', the houseproud Miss Warren scrubbing her step with scented toilet soap, the silent men leaning against the factory wall in collarless linen shirts and silk mufflers, cigarette burning so low it must surely scorch their lips. . . . In this street there was always such a feeling of permanency, so great a sense of following a long-established and deeply rooted pattern of living, that it seems impossible for the street to have been evacuated without inflicting the cruellest blow against its inhabitants and their lives.

A little pale sunshine breaks obliquely through the clouds and some facets of the chapel's buckled leaded lights shine. Here and there a few old women appear on the front doorsteps in clean Sunday pinafores. 'Blows up chilly', and they think of the times when the sun shone without interruption from

Easter until the end of October, and of the Long Sunday after-
noons on the warm pavement with a newspaper over their face
and the desultory talk across the street while the hot east wind
carried away eddies of dust down the road and the slate roofs
shone like glass in the fierce sunlight.

For a moment they see the street restored to that time of
long Sunday afternoons, with the tar melting in the road and
the curtains drawn as if for the dead against the sun. There is
once again the smell of cooking greens indistinguishable from
the smell of the drains where the children play in defiance of
their mothers' threats of the fever – memory of diptheria or
typhoid that had sent their brothers or friends to the 'pitty-
hole' a generation before. The thirsty old women in worn-
down grimacing carpet-slippers shuffle to the Off Licence with
a chipped enamel jug, and some children walk carefully to the
bakehouse bearing a huge metal tray of potatoes for cooking.

Then the long afternoon silence, sleeping off the beer and
the Sunday dinner. The women fall asleep on the front doorstep with the after-dinner peppermint burning their tongue.
Even on the side of the street that lies in shadow it's too hot to
move. The moisture begins to trickle down the faces of those
asleep in the sun, and even the children have fallen quiet,
pressing their faces against the cool stone doorsteps. A church
clock strikes three and somewhere a woman's voice is raised in
petulant recrimination against a husband who has only just
appeared for his Sunday dinner. Mrs B. blinks at a blowfly that
has settled on her cheek, and looking up across the street she
notices that little Mavis Coles isn't wearing any knicks. She
thinks it's scandalous, the way they treat that kid, but is too
tired to say so. Her baby starts to complain of the heat so she
gives him a thin arrowroot biscuit to suck. Dopey Freda is
chalking cabalistic signs on the walls. The other children won't
have anything to do with her, although with her pale lank hair
under that beret she might be a real child.

> Yum-yum, pig's bum,
> I'm gonnav a party
> And you can't come.

When they have finished the washing-up more of them emerge from the dim, cool passageways. Summer dresses that hang down six inches lower in front than at the back, bare red arms, legs mottled by long evenings at the fireside last winter. Granny Bray sits with her hands folded over her best blue pinafore. 'Oo's blew orf?' she asks, sniffing the air. 'It's the drains,' murmurs her next-door neighbour in her sleep. Joe Fenton's Maudie goes bleating down the street. She's never learnt to talk like other people's children – her mother was chased by a goat during her pregnancy. A distant sound of singing from Spring Lane Sunday School:

> Over the sea there are little brown children,
> Fathers and mothers and babies dear.
> No one has told them the Lord Jesus loves them,
> No one has told them that He is near.

'Finds you, this heat, dunnit?'

'Couldn't very well miss you, your size, dear.'

In the general store Mrs Taylor is having trouble. 'The damn cat's had its kittens in the dolly mixtures. At fivepence a quarter, if you please.' And she wonders how many of the spoiled sweets she can salvage, justifying herself with a 'They say we all eat a peck of dirt before we die.' Even if it's the afterbirth of a cat. 'First thing in the morning I know where I'm gooin'. I'm gooin' straight down to 'ave the bloody thing done in.'

'Oo no you ain't, woman,' says her husband from the depths of his armchair. 'I get a damn sight more affection out that cat than I'm ever got out o' you, I'll see you done in first.' But Mrs Taylor has already got the kettle on the boil for the kittens.

Charlie Rappitt watches the children in the gutter, and he thinks of the time when he had two legs as straight as theirs. He thinks of the years he unloaded beer barrels from the brewery dray, and of the wedge that snapped one day from its rusty chain underneath the high iron-rimmed wheel, the great barrels dancing and lurching on the cobbles that only came to rest as they struck his body against the brown stone wall.

The sun is for a moment obscured by a light cloud, and a shadow rushes down the street. Granny Bray shivers in spite of the heat at a sudden unwelcome memory. 'Killed in action.' A day like this. And she looks up and wonders if they see the same clouds in France.

On the pavement, on a felt stair-mat, sits Sam Wykes, an old man of ninety, and as he talks of his earliest memories he creates a world of people who exist on his authority alone, people born nearly two centuries ago. He is the demiurge who summons them from the dead with the slow incantatory inflexions of his rasping country voice: 'I can still see my old Pap, ole Pap Tonks, see 'im now I can' – and his listeners look round fearfully, as if they expect Pap Tonks himself to be born of a shaft of sunlight that has settled on the old man's boot, or to appear in the gloomy passage from behind the rust-coloured velvet curtain – 'I can see 'im with 'is peg-leg, an' I useder goo down there of a Sat'day mornin' without fail and clean it wi' goose-grease. 'E useder gi' me a penny for doin' it, so's it was ready to goo to church on Sunday, and that was when a penny really wor a penny.... Anyroad, I went down there one mornin' and the minute I turned the corner I knoo sommat were up – there was a stillness all about such as I'd never see of a Sat'day, and when I got to the 'ouse I seen the curtains was drawn, and I knoo it wadn't for the sun 'cause the sky were that low and broody it might a-bin the middle o' winter.... 'E'd bin took bad in the night and afore it were light 'e'd drew 'is last breath ... They'd laid 'im out in the parlour an' they told me I 'adn't gotter goo in there, but I waited while nobody wadn't watchin' an' then I nipped in to 'ave a look at 'im.... 'E looked lovely, 'cause they reckon the youth comes back to your cheek twenny-four hour arter yer dead, just as if 'e were asleep, but 'e looked a bit too much at peace to be still in this life. 'E were a gret fine man, weighed gettin' on for twenty stun, an' there 'e laid with 'is arms a-folded on 'is chest an' 'oldin' the Bible open in 'is 'ands....'

Sam Wykes evokes the life of the fields and the countryside, which persists in the memory of the street as the remembrance of its true origin sometimes returns to an unhappy stepchild.

He recalls the summers when even the wells dried up and the brown grass burst into flame in the heat of the sun and the leaves hung limp and grey with dust on the trees. He gives back to the wild flowers in the woods the names of a hundred years ago – mollyblobs and tittybottles, silverpennies and smell-smocks, gosling-grass and lord-and-ladies, as though the loss of these names among the streets and factories had taken from the flowers themselves something of the whiteness of the daisies and the dazzling uncertain contour of the marsh-mari-gold blooms. He keeps alive the memory of the beggars' barm running in the overflowing ditches, the bluebells almost white for lack of sun in Badby woods, the feeling of almost physical pain induced by the sight of the poppies they called blind-eyes dancing in the August cornfields. . . .

Mrs Fudge, fresh from her afternoon sleep, is splashing cold water in the chipped enamel bowl that stands in the low glazed stone sink and singing:

> Got no mansion, got no yacht,
> Still I'm happy with what I've got.
> I've got the sun in the morning
> And the moon at night.

'Come on, our Rosemary,' she calls shrilly, 'we're gooin' up yer Auntie Doll's.' And she licks a corner of her pinafore and wipes the child's sticky lollipop-stained face. A clean ribbon in her hair, and then off down the street to where Doll is waiting with her American boy-friend and a spread such as you didn't see once in a blue moon. Mrs Fudge didn't know how Doll coped, but then, ask no questions and you'll hear no lies was her motto, and it warmed the cockles of your heart to see the little girl's eyes light up at the piles of candy and tinned hams and peaches and chocolate biscuits. There couldn't be much wrong with the way it was come by if it made a child so happy. . . .

Now the hottest part of the day is over there is a little more movement.

'Do you want some clean socks, Sid?'

'No, 's all right, these'll do.'

'Oo no, they wun't, we ain't gooin' up our Maud's of a Sunday wi' your cheesy feet stinkin' the place out.'

Granny Bray's daughter waves to her from the top of the street. 'Yoo-oo.'

'I don't wanner goo an' see Gran.'

'Shh! She'll 'ear yer.'

' 'Ello, me duck,' she cries, as soon as she recognizes them. 'I wondered if you'd be a-comin'. She draws little Diane to her and kisses her with a noisy wet kiss. Diane moves away and surreptitiously wipes her face. Gran smells. Not dirty or anything. Just old. Gran goes inside and fetches a chair for her daughter. She seeks out a greasy pack of playing cards and teaches Diane to play draw-the-well-dry. Diane cheats, but she knows she's safe – the old lady can't see well enough to catch her out.

The breeze is a little stronger now. Mavis Coles feels the dust in her face and she shields herself with her arm, as she has learnt to do from her father's blows.

Mrs Hitchcock fans herself with the *Sunday Express* and silently hates the street and the flies and the heat and the crying children and the gossiping old women, and she thanks God she got her Denise through to the Notre Dame with the elocution and tennis and the better class of girl you get there. Freda peers round the jitty. She puts out a tongue stained with raspberry drops at Mrs Hitchcock and calls 'Old Mother Scratch-arse! Old Mother Scratch-arse!' and disappears again.

'That girl ought to be Put Away.'

'Well, you can bet your boots she never made that up by herself. She's heard the old hen crow.' And Mrs Hitchcock glares at the closed door of Number Ten, where Freda's mother sits talking to her visitors from the Other Side.

Tea. The jelly that didn't set properly because of the heat, the piece of ham that turned out to be nearly all gristle, the tin of salmon they all swore was coloured cod, Gran's dry seed-cake that Diane furtively slips behind the curtain.

Evening. The sun falling into Rube Warren's chimney pot. The sound of a piano through the open windows of 'The Gari-baldi', the thud of a heavy-bodied moth against a dusty win-

dow-pane. The light lingers on the brown stone façade of the
Church School with its windows pointed like hands in prayer,
its rows of low carved benches and lines of jam-jars filled
with buttercups. The evening is warmed by the heat of the
sun, caught up in the brick during the day and given back
to the cooling air after sunset. The silence is broken by the
screams of Mavis Coles, surprised by her mother in the hen-
coop showing her belly-button to a group of open-mouthed
children and frightening them with tales about its origin.
The tap-tap of her mother's high heels on the garden path,
the hurried though not quite quick enough pulling up of
a pair of navy-blue knickers, the slaps round the legs and Mrs
Coles' voice raised for everybody in the street to hear 'You
dirty little hound', while her audience struggle pell-mell
through the aperture in the wire netting and run away down
the street sucking the long red rusty scratches. There is the
scrape of a chair along the pavement, the slamming of a window, community hymn-singing on the radio.

'Bit cooler now.'

So they collect up the abandoned knitting and crumpled
newspapers and bags of sticky unwrapped sweets, and soon the
street is empty. Only Freda is left in the jitty, hugging a stray
cat and saying 'Red sky at night shepherd's delight.' But she
presses the cat too tightly – it suddenly spits and draws its
claws across her face leaving three parallel red grooves on her
cheek, and leaps away into the darkness. . . .

But they have gone from the streets now. It wasn't simply
that Vera put her head with all its noises in the gas-oven, it
wasn't Charlie Rappitt's big funeral with 'At the going down of
the sun' in the Deaths Column and the black board nailed over
the window. It wasn't simply that one day they told Freda she
was going for a nice long holiday in a lovely red house with
towers in the country. It wasn't that one September afternoon
Ellen Youl lay dead under the plum tree in the back garden
while the ripe fruit fell and burst around her on the grey slate
garden path. With them disappeared a sense of certainty in
their allegiance to a single received and unchallenged way of

life, the feeling that their life, the life of these streets was the only possible human life, and that everything else was spurious, unreal, lies. . . .

The few old women who still gather on the doorstep have lived to see the frightened neighbour carried out of her house, helpless under a red hospital blanket. They have seen the fissures appear in the masonry of the chapel where they still declare that they envy not the rich their joys and covet not the earth's glittering toys. They have watched the paint blister and the foundations sink, as the ground sinks above coffins that have rotted and collapsed. They have lived to hear the rats scratch at the wainscot of the house carefully preserved for their children, and to see the straw spread outside Charlie Rappitt's window during his long illness to muffle the footsteps of passers-by who had already disappeared.

They have lived to see their customs and rituals fall into desuetude, their accredited beliefs spent, their received ideas suddenly used up, as though in a decade they had passed through some vertiginous and incomprehensibly accelerated lifetime, and when they handed on to their children the only life they knew, enshrined in the family treasures now abandoned, the children laughed and refused them and went their ways.

The houses in which they took such pride appear suddenly ugly and shameful. Unfit for human habitation. Who then had lived here for four generations? They nod to a neighbour across the street and strain their ears for snatches of a hymn borne away on the cold wet wind. Bewildered, they return to the parlour, small insecure enclave of the past with its brass-studded armchairs, bamboo-framed cabinet and unplayed piano. In the dusty glass of 'The Raising of Lazarus' that covers nearly half the wall they see reflected the metal neck of a great predatory crane two streets away, and they are afraid. It is as though the new buildings and everything they signify are being fashioned at their expense, created out of their very substance, out of the breaches that appear daily in the once permanent and immutable structures of the crumbling terraces. They surround themselves with the familiar things, and fetch out the precious shoe-box full of commemorative relics, the sad photographs of rickety children and consumptive brides and soldiers smiling before they died, samplers and antimacassars and wall-texts of 'God is Love' worked in Gothic lettering that stands out in red twine fierce as a threat. Just as they have carefully preserved the single bloom from their wedding bouquet pressed between the pages of the Book of Psalms, as they have carefully husbanded the fruits of summer in the rows of Kilner jars on the cellar steps, so they have kept alive an obsolete way of life in the musty exhalations of wax tulips and dusty plush and faded velvet and sunbleached lace. And they have clung to their superseded beliefs as an old tramp will cling to a threadbare overcoat, hugging it closer to himself for warmth and comfort as the season changes, until it finally becomes his winding-sheet.

Now that those they loved have died or gone away from the street, all the ideas and beliefs, the customs and traditions shared and associated with them seem less necessary, less relevant. Because parents or husbands had been so involved in a certain pattern of living, they had accepted it too, but now that all kinsfolk have gone they are stranded, isolated and helpless. They are exposed to an overwhelming sense of loss, seeing the certainties of a lifetime take on a bewildering and terrifying relativity. They are brought into rude contact with other kinds of life, people and things from which they had always been separated: the Jamaicans dancing and singing and clapping in a street that had never heard anything more outlandish than a discordant piano in 'The Garibaldi' or aunts at family celebrations singing 'The Last Rose of Summer' or 'Don't Go Down the Mine, Daddy', the boy who brings home mysterious books of foreign languages and suspect volumes of poetry to the mother who as a child had seen nothing more than an encyclopedia bought from a door-to-door salesman to reinforce an unsteady table-leg, and who had once been slapped by her father for consulting it for its educational content, the son who arrives in a Wolseley every Sunday afternoon to take an old woman to see a sister whom she had not visited for forty years, when she had travelled half a day in a slow and bumpy carrier's cart.

The life of the streets had a devitalizing effect, and did not allow of any departure from a rigidly fixed pattern of behaviour and relationships. The change from country to street life did not involve so radical a modification of their values as is sometimes believed. Each generation learned more from its predecessor than from any other source, and in spite of the hiatus in environment – perhaps even because of it – they turned for reassurance and instruction to those people and things that were familiar to them. The force and conviction of the life they had always known carried them over four or five generations, and there was no loss of continuity, no collapse in the transmission of ideas. For any society whose members derive significance from its values has an unassailable source of strength (which it sometimes mistakenly assumes to be a source of truth as well). It is only within the last generation that the breakdown has occurred among the old in the dying streets. They are like a race of people disturbed in their allegiance to infallible deities by missionaries who assure them that their gods are blasphemous and obscene. They are shown the error and irrelevance of their faith by those who have access to greater truths, and who tear the veils from the eyes of others, veils that prove to be not veils at all, but living membranes, the removal of which leaves nothing but empty and bleeding sockets.